DATE DUE			

LINGUISTIC REPRESENTATION

PHILOSOPHICAL STUDIES SERIES IN PHILOSOPHY

VOLUME 1

JAY F. ROSENBERG

University of North Carolina

LINGUISTIC

REPRESENTATION

D. REIDEL PUBLISHING COMPANY

DORDRECHT-HOLLAND / BOSTON-U.S.A.

Library of Congress Cataloging in Publication Data

Rosenberg, Jay F
    Linguistic representation.

    (Philosophical studies series in philosophy ; v. 1)
    Bibliography: p.
    Includes index.
    1. Languages—Philosophy. I. Title.

P106.R59   401   74–26886
ISBN 90–277–0533–X

First printing: December 1974

Published by D. Reidel Publishing Company,
P.O. Box 17, Dordrecht, Holland

Sold and distributed in the U.S.A., Canada, and Mexico
by D. Reidel Publishing Company, Inc.
306 Dartmouth Street, Boston,
Mass. 02116, U.S.A.

Printed in Belgium

DEDICATION

I'd dedicate it to my wife, but we're divorced.

I'd dedicate it to my daughter, but she can't
read it yet.

So this one is for Wilfrid Sellars, to show
him what, if one isn't careful, can come of
talking philosophy to someone who listens.

MOTTO

"Again, those are called Nominalists who show diligence and zeal in understanding all the properties of terms on which the truth or falsity of a sentence depends, and without which the perfect judgment of the truth or falsity of propositions cannot be made. These properties are: supposition, appellation, ampliation, restriction, exponible distribution. They especially understand obligations and the nature of the insoluble, the true foundation of dialectical arguments and of their failure. Being instructed in these things, they easily understand concerning any given argumentation whether it is good or bad."

— Letter from the Nominalist masters
of the University of Paris
to King Louis XI, 1473

CONTENTS

PREFACE

This book is nominally about linguistic representation. But, since it is we who do the representing, it is also about us. And, since it is the universe which we represent, it is also about the universe. In the end, then, this book is about everything, which, since it is a philosophy book, is as it should be.

I recognize that it is nowadays unfashionable to write books about everything. Philosophers of language, it will be said, ought to stick to writing about language; philosophers of science, to writing about science; epistemologists, to writing about knowing; and so on. The real world, however, perversely refuses to carve itself up so neatly, and, although I recognize that the real world is nowadays also unfashionable, in the end I judged that one might get closer to the truth of various matters by going along with it. So I have done so.

It was Wilfrid Sellars who initially convinced me of the virtues of this way of proceeding. At this point one normally says something like "The debt that this book owes him is immense". I would say it too, were it not to understate the case. From Wilfrid, I learned to *think* about things. If the upshot of my thinking tends, as it obviously does, to show a general consilience with the upshot of his, it is primarily because he is so *very* good at it — and he had a head start.

While paying debts, I feel constrained to mention a few other names. The reader who knows my work will recognize this book as the culmination of several years' studies in which the young Wittgenstein figures prominently. So this book has Tractarian roots. But it is not a book about the *Tractatus* (except insofar as it is about everything), and I shall not develop even my essentially Tractarian theses by *talking* about the *Tractatus*. To do so is dialectical suicide. I'd like to say that I was clever enough to figure that out for myself, but I wasn't. My friend Paul Churchland pointed it out to me one cold night in Winnipeg, and thereby established his lifetime right to be listened to.

A debt of equal magnitude is owed my chairman W.D. Falk ('David', to his friends) for being so adept at juggling the departmental chaos as to arrange for me a semester without classroom responsibilities. As this benighted institution has never seen fit to institute a program of sabbaticals,

David's was a less minor contribution than it might initially seem to the more fortunate among you.

There is a melange of colleagues and graduate students to whom I owe a more diffuse debt. This book is probably less obscure than it could easily have been. If it is, it is mostly because these colleagues and students perversely refused to understand what I meant until I said it. This is, perhaps, not a good tactic to pursue in casual conversation, but in philosophy it turns out to be a cardinal virtue, and I am lucky to count my friends among the virtuous.

While this book has Tractarian roots, it is not Tractarian root and branch. Partly, this is because the *Tractatus* is a book wholly without an epistemology, and it doesn't work without one. Mostly, however, this is because I have changed my mind about the picture theory. It is, perhaps, rare for a philosopher to change his mind, but it is unfortunately even rarer for one to admit it. And this is understandable. Nevertheless, I feel constrained to do so. Some of you may think you know where I stand on certain matters. And you have every reason to think so. But you'd better read the book. I sometimes don't stand there any more.

My colleague, Paul Ziff, once wrote a book called *Semantic Analysis* in the Preface to which he enjoined the reader, were he to come across something to all appearances obviously false, stupid, or nonsensical, seriously to entertain the hypothesis that Ziff meant exactly what he said. Even the cleverest and best-intentioned persons occasionally say things which are obviously false, stupid, or nonsensical. His injunction, of course, did no good, for a variety of commentators proceeded to remark in great detail on what he "must have meant". It applies, however, to this book as well, and, since I am somewhat enamored of the innocent Quixotic gesture, I thought that I'd mention it.

And here is the point at which one thanks the loyal and diligent typist. Well, I typed it myself, and I am everlastingly grateful to me for it.

University of North Carolina at   JAY. F. ROSENBERG
Chapel Hill

April, 1973

CHAPTER I

REPRESENTATION AND LANGUAGE

The essential and characteristic human activity is representation — that is, the production and manipulation of representations. Except for the new-born and the severely brain-damaged, all humans, of whatever time and culture, engage in it, and, insofar as we can now say with any confidence (the verdict on dolphins and the data on Martians not yet having come in), only humans do.

'Representation' I mean to construe broadly. Phenomenologically, it is either iconic or symbolic; logically, I hope to argue, it is all of a piece. Except as it can illuminate the linguistic mode, I shall have little to say about iconic representation. Its traditional home is in the plastic, visual, arts. A representation is iconic if, as we say, it *resembles* that which it *represents*. But these are difficult and opaque notions, and so we should not take too much to be clarified by formulas of that sort. Iconic representation ranges from the Lascaux cave-paintings to Warhol's soup cans. It includes portraiture, still-life, and commemorative sculpture, and, so it not be thought essentially visual, it includes as well the whistling of the last move-ment of Beethoven's Ninth Symphony for a friend to remind him of how it goes.

Symbolic representation is, paradigmatically, linguistic representation. The class, of course, is broader, including systems of hieroglyphics, codes, ciphers, musical notation, maps, graphs, and charts, but it is language, I shall argue, which is logically primary and it is language which will be my prin-cipal concern. With language we can say how the world is; and we can say how the world *isn't* — and both of these *in absentia* from that in the world of which we speak. I want to understand how this is possible.

A system of representation allows of two different sorts of activity: representation of *things* and representation of *states of affairs.* In language this becomes the time-honored distinction between naming and saying. Linguistic representation of things is naming or reference or denotation. I shall need a special term to mark this job in language, and 'designation' seems currently to carry as little initial theoretical load as any. So I shall call the *linguistic* representation of things 'designation' and the bits of language which are its vehicles will be 'designators'.

The vehicle of linguistic representation of states of affairs, on the other hand, is the (declarative) sentence. Language, of course, is manifold in its uses – as the famous Wittgensteinian catalogue (*PI*, Section #23) reminds us: commanding, describing, reporting, story telling, asking, thanking, cursing, greeting, praying, and so on *ad*, perhaps, *infinitum*. I, however, am concerned with but *one* function of language, the making of matter-of-factual claims about the empirical world, for I am interested in language only as a system of representations. Thus what I wish to isolate in language is that job variously called 'saying' or 'stating' or 'asserting', and I shall need a technical term to mark it as well. I shall call it 'claiming' and the bits of language which are its vehicles will thus become 'claims'. I think this is the central function and its possibility a necessary precondition of any of the others, but I shall not pause here to argue for that point.

What I want to focus on, then, is designation and claiming. And I shall begin by asking what requirements must be met by an adequate theory of language as a representational system. What are the particular and characteristic features of a language which must be accounted for by any such theory?

The most striking feature of language has already been remarked upon. It is the fact that language can be used to talk about the world. In this use, language is *intersubjective*. It is a medium of *communication*. And this imposes several constraints upon any adequate account of language.

For one thing, in order to function as an effective medium of communication, language must be *finitely learnable*. In fact, languages are acquired with remarkable speed. A child typically has a full working command of his native language well before age five. True, there are nuances which will not be sorted out until much later, and an immense account of vocabulary remains to be acquired (although a surprising amount has already been acquired), but a child of five is equipped to carry on a relatively sophisticated and fully intelligible conversation about the world in which he moves. Any theory of language must show how this is possible.

More remarkably still, a speaker learns his native language without being *taught* it. As Ziff puts it:

... one is not taught one's native language, one learns it. In our culture a child is not taught to speak at school: he can speak before he goes to school. If he cannot, he is not likely to be taught much at school. If he can speak before he goes to school, who taught him to speak? The parent who teaches his child an occasional word may think he is teaching his child to speak. But a normal person during the early part of his life learns a thousand words a year, more than three words a day on the average. Who teaches him these words? (*SA*, 35)

It is, in fact, sufficient simply for an infant to grow up in a speaking mileau. If a child is among speakers of a language and is spoken to in that language, then, unless he is badly brain-damaged, he will learn to speak that language. An adequate theory of language, then, must account for this: Language is *finitely learnable without teaching.*

What a child has acquired when he has learned a language is a vocabulary and a pair of competences. Vocabulary items are learned individually, but claims are not. Most of what a native speaker says has not been said before. And, correlatively, most of what a native speaker hears, he has not heard before. The native speaker of a language has, then, a pair of abilities or competences. He has, first, the ability to produce new claims, claims which have not been made before, neither by him nor, indeed, by any other speaker of his — or any other — language. He has, in other words, a *creative production competence for claims*, and this is one striking fact about language for which any adequate theory must account. In addition, the native speaker of a language has the ability to understand new claims framed in that language, claims which he has not made and which have not been put to him before. He has, in other words, a *creative recognition competence for claims*, and this is another striking fact about language for which an adequate theory must account.

It follows immediately, I suggest, that language must be an *essentially combinatorial* system. A claim must be logically complex; it must have *parts*. And what claim it is must be a function of, must depend on — and only on —, what those parts are and how they are arranged. Only in this way could a finitely acquired language form the basis for the production and recognition of a potentially infinite number of distinct claims articulated in that language. Thus a claim will necessarily have *constituents*, and there will be some correct *count* of them. That is, there will be a *parsing* of the claim which explains what claim it is by virtue of an enumeration of its constituents and a commentary upon their properties and interrelationships. That is what is wrong with arguments such as this (drawn from Pitcher's critique of classical correspondence theories of truth):

There is a foreign language — I have just invented it — in which the proposition we express by saying "The cat is on the mat" is expressed by the one-word sentence "Catamat". Are we to say that when a speaker of this new language says "Catamat" he is expressing a proposition with only one constituent? But then how could that be the same proposition as the one we express by saying "The cat is on the mat", since ours has three constituents? (*IT*,12–3)

The proper response to this gambit is to put Pitcher's powers of invention to the test. He claims to have invented a foreign *language* – say, Pitcherese. How, then, does one claim in Pitcherese that the cat is near or under the mat, that the dog is on the mat or on the log, or that the cat is on the floor or on the log? Is the resemblance of 'catamat' to our English sentence merely coincidental, or does Pitcherese yield up such further one-word sentences as 'catemat', 'catumat', 'dogamat', 'dogalog', 'catafloor', and 'catalog' to make these cousin claims? If Pitcherese is genuinely a language – that is, if it satisfies the requirements of finite learnability, creative production competence, and creative recognition competence – then the answer must surely be that it does. It follows, too, that we must carefully distinguish the count of *words of a sentence* from the count of *constituents of a claim* (in Pitcher's terminology: from the count of the constituents of the proposition which we express by means of the sentence). Indeed, Pitcher himself implicitly grants this distinction. 'Catamat' he counts as expressing a one-constituent proposition on the grounds that it is a one-word sentence, but the proposition expressed by 'The cat is on the mat' has, he says, *three* constituents, and this despite the fact that the sentence 'The cat is on the mat' has *six* words.

The count of words in a sentence is a *structural* count. It depends only upon the pattern of printers' spaces in the sentence, a pattern which need bear no uniform or simple relation to the jobs being done by the various bits of the sentence. The count of constituents of a claim, on the other hand, is a *functional* count. *It* depends precisely upon the contributions which bits of the sentence make to determining what claim\the sentence as a whole makes. One should be reminded here of certain passages from the *Tractatus*:

3.143   Although a propositional sign is a fact, this is obscured by the usual form of expression in writing or print.

For in a printed proposition, for example, no essential difference is apparent between a propositional sign and a word.

4.032   Even the proposition, *Ambulo*, is composite: for its stem with a different ending yields a different sense, and so does its ending with a different stem.

While these passages address the point which I have just been making, what is in addition particularly noteworthy about them is their apparent conflation of propositions with propositional *signs*. For Wittgenstein here speaks of "printed propositions" which have "stems" and "endings". Elsewhere in the *Tractatus*, he is quite explicit about the identification:

3.12   ... a proposition is a propositional sign in its projective relation to the world.

In terms of our discussion of Pitcher's argument, we can now understand this point as well, for it should now be clear that there is no *ontological* distinction marked by the differentiation of sentences and claims. Talk about a sentence (which I shall always use in the sense of 'sentence token') and talk about the claim it makes are two kinds of *talk* about one *object* — an inscription; a pile of ink, graphite, or chalk. Both modes of discourse have a single subject matter and claims are as "in the world", as much a part of the natural order, as sentences. For claims *are* sentences, functionally described. Sellars has a convenient phrase for marking this single subject matter. He calls them (*T&C*, 212) "natural linguistic objects" — 'natural' to highlight their home in an empirical ontology, and 'linguistic' to mark them as fit subjects for functional claim-descriptions. I shall, where useful, adopt this terminology as well.

While a person's linguistic resources are finite (since finitely learned), the potentialities for their deployment are infinite; while one's own linguistic experiences are unique, one's potentialities for speaking and understanding are shared. These facts, we have seen, mark language as essentially combinatorial. They have been taken as well to mark it as essentially *rule-governed*. The great strength of the advocates of linguistic rules has always been this: That it is utterly unintelligible how diverse speakers of a language can make and understand claims which have not been made before unless we grant that the speakers have in common a set of *rules* for making and understanding claims. Only in this way could finite resources be *uniformly* projected into infinite combinatorial possibilities.

This is the heart of the case for linguistic rules. But there is a case against them as well. At least language does not appear, *prima facie*, to be a rule-*constituted* activity.

We may take such a game as chess to be our paradigm of a rule-constituted activity. The difficulty is that speaking a language looks more like pursuing a teleological activity than like playing such a game. What I am calling 'teleological activity' is activity directed toward getting something done, activity which is means toward some end. Using a tool for its designed, intended, purpose is a convenient paradigm of a teleological activity. Ziff exploits this paradigm in his critique of the rule-constituted view of language:

It is possible to misuse words, or to use them correctly or incorrectly; e.g. philosophers who speak of "the rules of language" (or of "moral rules") are I believe misusing the word 'rule'. But I do not think they are breaking any rules. It is possible to misuse a screwdriver, to use it correctly or incorrectly: are there rules for using screwdrivers? This too would be an odd use of the word. (*SA*, 35)

Within a game of chess, there is much teleological activity. Each move is directed toward the end of checkmating the opposing king. Chess itself, however — the playing of the game — is most frequently engaged in, as we say, for its own sake, as an *autotelic* activity rather than as a teleological one. The majority of utterances of a language are teleological, aiming at informing, warning, persuading, intimidating, insulting, requesting, and the like — what I shall call illocutionary and perlocutionary ends. Of course, there are autotelic linguistic activities as well. Much poetry, although not all, will fall under this head. What Ziff is calling attention to is the way in which these categories interact with the notion of a rule.

There are two sorts of mismoves one can make at chess. One sort impedes the teleological. Leaving one's queen *en prise*, for example, is poor chess — but it is still chess. Not so with what we term a violation of a chess rule. If one begins moving rooks diagonally, and persists after correction, one has *a fortiori* ceased to play chess. It is not just that the teleological activity has been impeded. The autotelic activity has been suspended. Presumed rules of language, Ziff is claiming, behave more like the strategical principles of sound teleological chess than like the rule-constraints of autotelic chess. To deviate significantly from the norm in language is to fail to be understood, to fail to inform, warn, intimidate, or what have you. But it is not to cease speaking or even to cease speaking, say, English. It may, in fact, be precisely to pursue autotelic linguistic activity. Thus, there is even English nonsense poetry. Contrast, for example, the English:

> 'Twas brillig, and the slithy toves
> Did gyre and gimble in the wabe:
> All mimsy were the borogoves,
> And the mome raths outgrabe.

with the German:

> Es brillig war. Die schlichte Toven
> Wirrten und wimmelten in Waben;
> Und aller-mümsige Burggoven
> Die mohmen Räth' ausgraben.

and the French:

> Il brilgue: les tôves lubricilleux
> Se gyrent en vrillant dans le guave,
> Enmimés sont les gougebosqueux,
> Et le mômerade horsgrave.

This is another linguistic phenomenon which stands in need of an account. Let us call it *"free deviation from the norm"*. It suggests that, if the notion of a rule enters at all into a correct account of linguistic representation, it will do so in a way different from the way in which it enters into an account of such games as chess. The matter is a complex one and stands in need of adjudication. Its details, and its resolution, will form the substance of a succeeding chapter.

There is a second sort of deviation permitted by systems of linguistic representation, deviation from truth. It is, in other words, possible to claim what is not the case, to make false claims. Correlatively, it is possible to claim *truly* that something *is* not the case. Call this the *possibility of representing falsehoods*. Traditionally, it has given rise to the metaphysical problems of not-being and, more generally, to much ado about 'nothing'. Thus Parmenides: "Thou canst not *know* that which is not (for that is impossible) nor *utter* it." I shall eschew, of course, the problem of not-being − and Parmenidean and Heideggerian metaphysics in general − but the possibility of representing falsehoods stands in need of an account, and providing one is a further requirement of an adequate theory of linguistic representation.

The last fact about language which needs to be mentioned is that, as our plurality of Jabberwockys indicates, there is not one language but a multiplicity of languages. Within limits, it is possible to translate from one of these languages into another. Nor is translation between modes of representation limited to languages. It is possible to *say* what a picture or sculpture represents, and, for many journeys, a set of verbal instructions will do as well as a map. What the limits of translation are, of course, is both debatable and hotly debated. One obvious set of constraints those of nuance. In general, the more teleological a linguistic selection, the more readily it can cross the gap between diverse languages. Technical essays 'in scientific journals, aimed at informing, translate more readily than literary prose; literary porse passages, with greater facility than poetry. Conversely, the difficulty of translation increases as perlocutionary ends grade off from informing to the evocation of various affective and conative states.

These, of course, are limitations in practice. But there may be limitations in principle as well. Most familiarly, Quine has argued the existence of severe epistemological limitations to the enterprise of translation − his thesis of the indeterminacy of radical translation and its extension as the problem of the inscrutability of reference. An adequate theory of linguistic representation, then, must address the question of to what extent interlinguistic translation is possible and must offer some account of the epistemology of that enterprise.

I arrive, then, at seven constraints on an adequate theory of linguistic representation, seven questions for such a theory to answer:

1. How is it possible for language to represent the world? How does a system of linguistic representations secure extra-linguistic import?
2. How is a language learned without being taught?
3. How is it possible for a language user to make new claims? (Creative production competence for claims)
4. How is it possible for a language user to understand new claims? (Creative recognition competence for claims)
5. How is it possible for a language user freely to deviate from the norms of his language without ceasing thereby to be a user of that language?
6. How is it possible to make false claims, and to truly claim that something is not the case?
7. What are the limits and epistemology of inter-linguistic translation?

We might, in fact, say that a language *is* a representational system which is finitely learnable, intersubjective and open-ended in production and recognition, allows of free deviation, permits the representation of falsehoods, and is, within some limits, translatable into other systems of representation both linguistic and non-linguistic. If we do, my principal question can be given a Kantian tone: How is linguistic representation in general possible?

Linguistic representation is, however, only one species of symbolic representation. At times, then, I shall be addressing the broader question: How is symbolic representation in general possible? In fact, I hope in the end to provide an answer to a still broader question: How is representation in general possible? For, I shall be arguing, all representation is logically of a piece. But that is getting far ahead of my story. The thing to do now is to begin.

CHAPTER II

A MENTALISTIC THEORY

It has become fairly commonplace nowadays to say that it is not bits of language which mean something but rather *people* who mean something by (their uses of) bits of language. Thus, Strawson tells us:

'Mentioning', or 'referring', is not something an expression does; it is something that someone can use an expression to do. (*OR*, 180)

and, analogously, one would expect to find:

'Asserting', or 'stating', is not something that a sentence does; it is something that someone can use a sentence to do.

'Reference' and 'assertion' (or 'statement') are thus, in the first instance, names for linguistic actions ("speech acts") – acts of refer*ring* or assert*ing* performed by persons. And talk about the meanings of *expressions* (pieces of language) is supposed to be derivative from talk about linguistic actions of these sorts.

To give the meaning of an expression... is to give general directions for its use to refer to or mention particular objects or persons; to give the meaning of a sentence is to give *general directions* for its use in making true or false assertions. (Strawson, *OR*, 181)

In the terminology which I have adopted, 'designating' and 'claiming' are held to label linguistic actions, and such schemata as

      (expression) x designates A

and

      (sentence) S claims that p

are to be viewed as (possibly very complex) functions of such schemata as

(agent, person) M *uses* x *to designate* A

and

      (agent, person) M *uses* S *to claim* that p

where 'to designate A' and 'to claim that p' are, in their primary sense, verbs of human *action* which take expressions designating linguistic agents, speakers, as their proper subjects.

Call this *agent-semantics*. Agent-semantics has as its root philosophical motivation the desire to account for language as a vehicle of communication. Language (in its overt forms as speech or writing) is seen primarily as an instrument for structuring the attention of an audience (a phrase which I owe to Paul Ziff). The *analysis* of such linguistic actions as referring or asserting, then, will make reference to the effects on hearers of *uses* of bits of language by speakers.

But what is a *use*? Strawson, for example, distinguishes among

(A1)   a sentence
(A2)   the use of a sentence [to assert, state, etc.]

and

(A3)   an utterance of a sentence

and, correlatively, among

(B1)   an expression
(B2)   the use of an expression [to refer, mention, etc.]

and

(B3)   an utterance of an expression

(*OR*, 179) *A* use in the sense of a *using* of an expression or sentence by a person is, like an utterance of an expression or sentence — and unlike the expression or sentence used — a datable event. Not so a use to which an expression or sentence may be put. According to Strawson, the principles for *counting* uses in this latter sense are not the same as the principles for counting utterances or usings:

... two men who simultaneously uttered the sentence ['The king of France is wise'] in the reign of Louis XIV made two different utterances of the same sentence, though they made the same *use* of the sentence. (*OR*, 180)

Wittgenstein's remark (*PI*, #43)

For a *large* class of cases — though not for all — in which we employ the word "meaning" it can be defined thus: the meaning of a word is its use in the language.

has, notoriously, given rise to a variety of "use-theories of meaning". One common interpretation of Wittgenstein's use of 'use' here has been Strawson's: the *use* to which a bit of language is put by a speaker on a given occasion is to be identified by specifying the linguistic act performed by the speaker on that occasion. On this construal, in other words, use-theory *is* agent-semantics. Thus, if we ask, for example, *what* use the two speakers in Strawson's example made of the sentence 'The king of France is wise', the answer will take the form:

They used the sentence (on that occasion) *to assert* that Louis XIV is wise (or: to assert of Louis XIV that he is wise).

and the uses of the component expressions 'the king of France' and 'is wise' are to perform, respectively, the linguistic actions of *referring* to Louis XIV and of *predicating* wisdom of him. *The* use of an expression or sentence (in general, and not on a particular occasion), then, will be some function of its possible *uses* by speakers on specific occasions. This is the theory which Alston had codified in his essay "Meaning and Use". Roughly,

'u' means $v =_{df}$ 'u' and 'v' can be substituted for each other... without changing the linguistic act potentials of... sentences. (*M&U*, 410)

The linguistic acts which Alston selects as determining "linguistic act potentials" are precisely the linguistic actions of agent-semantics. They are Austin's *illocutionary* acts. Austin marks off the illocutionary from the perlocutionary by a variety of distinctions (See *HDTW*, pp. 98–131) of which Alston selects three as crucial:

(1) It is a necessary condition for the performance of a perlocutionary, but not an illocutionary, act, that the utterance have had a certain sort of result [effect on its audience].

(2) A perlocutionary, but not an illocutionary, act can be performed without the use of language, or any other conventional device.

and

(3) Illocutionary acts are more fundamental than perlocutionary acts in the means-ends hierarchy. [Typically, one can illocute *in order to* perlocute, but not conversely.] (*M&U*, 411–2).

An *utterance* of an expression or sentence, on the other hand, is related to what Austin calls a *locutionary* act. As he parses it, performing a locutionary act is "saying something" in the "full normal sense" of that phrase, and this includes, by Austin's reckoning,

... the utterances of certain noises, the utterance of certain words in a certain construction, and the utterance of them with a certain 'meaning' in the favourite philosophical sense of that word, i.e. with a certain sense and with a certain reference. (*HDTW*, 94)

It should be clear, however, that this Austinian construal of "locutionary act" runs together matters which the Strawson-Alston view keeps separate. For in agent-semantics, "sense" and "reference" are explicitly attached, not to the *utterance* of an expression or sentence but to the *use* of the expression or sentence. The utterance of words "with a certain 'meaning' " is thus, on the Strawson-Alston construal, a matter of illocutionary rather than locutionary content. Thus not *all* utterances of sentences are assertions (questions, commands, requests, etc.) nor are all utterances of designators (ostensibly referring expressions) instances of referring. The identity conditions for utterances, in other words, are to be taken on the Strawson-Alston view as strictly *structural* — phonemic or graphemic — and the job of identifying the utterance ends when one has specified, in Austinian terms, the "certain words in a certain construction". Tape-recorders, parrots, and the like can thus issue utterances (although, to the extent that tape-recorders, say, are not *agents* we shall resist saying of them that they *utter* expressions or sentences).

To *use* a bit of language (an utterance), then, is to illocute — in a mildly extended sense of "illocutionary act" which adds to the "whole-sentence acts" of asserting, commanding, questioning, and so on the acts of referring and predicating as well — and *the use* of a bit of language, in general, is its illocutionary act potential. Now, as Strawson and Alston employ the terminology of agent-semantics, the verbs of illocutionary linguistic actions are, in Ryle's phrase, 'achievement verbs'; they

... signify not merely that some performance has been gone through, but also that something has been brought off by the agent going through it. They are verbs of success. (*CM*, 130)

Thus to say of an agent that he *referred* to a particular object on a particular occasion is to say that he *succeeded in referring* to that object on that occasion. To speak of success or failure, however, is to suppose that there is some aim, goal, purpose, or end-in-view the attaining of which *counts* as success and the failing to attain of which, as failure. Thus referring and asserting, as *tasks* which can be successfully or unsuccessfully performed by an agent, can be characterized with reference to their ends:

One of the main purposes for which we use language is the purpose of stating facts about things and persons and events. If we want to fulfil this purpose, we must have some way of forestalling the question, 'What (who, which one) are you talking about?' as well as the question, 'What are you saying about it (him, her)?'. The task of forestalling the first question is the referring (or identifying) task. The task of forestalling the second is the attributive (or descriptive or classificatory or ascriptive) task. (Strawson, *OR*, 187)

The success or failure of a linguistic action of referring or predicating or asserting is thus to be measured by its effects upon its audience. The actions themselves are illocutionary, but the intended effects, perlocutionary. Thus one refers in order to get one's audience to *pick out* or *identify* a particular object or person as the subject of discourse. And one states or asserts in order to get one's audience, say, to *believe* that so-and-so is the case. The success of the illocutionary act (referring, asserting) is thus a function of the success of the perlocutionary act (bringing it about that the audience picks out or identifies, bringing it about that the audience believes). Carried to its natural conclusion, this line of thought denies the possibility of performing illocutionary acts *at all* in the absence of any occasion for perlocutionary success (a position actually espoused by Aldrich. See *IS.*). Yet this is not Strawson's view, for it fails adequately to distinguish, as he attempts to, one's *succeeding in illocuting* from one's *illocuting successfully*, the bringing off of the *act* from the bringing off of its *end.*

It is Strawson's distinction between *securing* reference and *conveying* it which reflects these two dimensions of success. For one to have secured reference (referred), it is sufficient that he have issued an utterance while possessed of the relevant perlocutionary intentions. He must, in other words – to sound a theme which will become increasingly important as I proceed – *have something in mind* to which he intends to be referring and which he intends his audience to pick out or identify. This, parenthetically, is the root from which springs Strawson's doctrine of presupposing. If the speaker has no object in mind, if there is no object which he intends that his audience pick out or identify, then, on Strawson's view, he has failed to bring off an act of referring at all. Since stating consists of reference and predication, he fails, under these conditions, to bring off the more complex illocutionary act of stating as well. It is precisely here that "truth-value gaps" arise. If no stating has occurred, then no statement has been made. There is, in other words, no *candidate* for the ascription of truth or false-hood. It follows, then, that radical failure of reference entails, on Strawson's view, the complete absence of a truth-vehicle. What is *said* (not: stated) on such an occasion is neither true nor false.

Securing reference (referring), then, is not, properly speaking, a genuine achievement verb. It is, in this way, akin to *trying*. I may genuinely succeed or fail in what I am trying to achieve, but I cannot succeed or fail in the trying of it, for I cannot try to try. *Conveying* reference (referring success-fully), on the other hand, is an achievement in the full sense, for here the speaker attains the perlocutionary aim of his illocutionary act. He succeeds, in other words, in getting his audience to pick out or identify the particular object or person which he has in mind and thereby brings off, not only an illocutionary act, but a perlocutionary act as well.

The questions to be forestalled are *audience* questions, but the perlocutionary end is the *speaker's* aim. A speaker succeeds in forestalling the question "What are you talking about?", in other words, when he succeeds in bringing it about that his audience picks out or identifies *his* object of reference. To refer, then, is to utter an expression with the *intention* of bringing it about that the audience pick out or identify a particular object – the object which the speaker *intends* them to pick out. Similarly, to assert is to utter, typically, a sentence with the intention of bringing it about that the audience, say, come to believe something – something, in particular, which the speaker *intends* that they come to believe. In general, then, we have a reading for (illocutionary) *use*:

> To *use* an expression or sentence (to illocute) is to utter it with perlocutionary intent.

And an illocutionary linguistic action is successful when it in fact *has* the intended perlocutionary effect upon its audience.

Thus *intentions*, specifically the speaker's intentions, have moved to the center of our stage.

A theory which thus locates the conceptual underpinnings of an agent-semantics in speakers' intentions has been developed in some detail in recent years by H.P. Grice. Grice sees linguistic meaning as a species of what he terms 'non-natural meaning' (meaning-nn). He shares with the view which I have been explicating the notion that the end-in-view of language use is per-locutionary – the production of some effect in the audience – but, noting with Austin that perlocutionary aims may be accomplished by non-linguistic means, Grice attempts to ensure that it is the *conventional linguistic perfor-mance* of the speaker which is both intended by him to effect his per-locutionary aims and which, if his intentions are successfully executed, does effect those aims. Thus Grice imposes the further requirement that the speaker's intention be recognized by the audience and that this recognition be causally instrumental in bringing about the perlocutionary effects which the speaker intends, arriving at the schema:

"A meant-nn something by *x*" is (roughly) equivalent to "A intended the utterance of *x* to produce some effect in an audience by means of the recognition of this inten-tion". (*M*, 442)

What an *utterance*, x, means-nn, then, will be some complex

... statement or disjunction of statements about what "people" (vague) intend (with qualifications about "recognition") to effect by x. (*M*, 442)

Grice is primarily concerned with whole-sentence utterances, and the perlocutionary effects which he canvasses are consequently primarily a function of mood. In "Meaning", the end-in-view for an indicative utterance is taken to be that the audience believe what the speaker means-nn by the utterance to be true, but by the time of "Utterer's Meaning and Intentions" this had become refined to the production of the audience's belief that the *speaker* believes what he means-nn by his utterance.

Grice's theory is a theory of non-natural *meaning*, and I have basically eschewed talk of meaning in my development so far. The earlier equation of use-theory with agent-semantics, however, indicates how we should proceed. The fundamental Strawsonian whole-sentence schema was, recall,

(Agent) A uses (the sentence) S to assert that p.

This comes apart, I argued, into an utterance by A of the sentence S and the possession by A of the relevant perlocutionary intentions *vis-à-vis* his utterance and its effect on his audience. We are now in a position to expand on this account, for we may treat Grice's notion of non-natural meaning precisely as a refinement of the notion of a perlocutionary intention. Thus

A uses the sentence S to assert that p

will be roughly equivalent to

A utters the sentence S *and* A means-nn by his utterance of S that p

and, in full contemporary Gricean dress, to

A utters S *and*

A intends his utterance of S to produce in his audience a certain belief (viz: that A believes that p) by means of their recognition of that intention.

What of

A uses the expression x to refer to O,

the other Strawsonian schema? Grice, I have already noted, considers explicitly only whole-sentence utterances, but the Gricean scheme

A intends his utterance of x to produce some effect in his audience by means of the recognition of that intention.

will fit fragmentary expressions as well as whole sentences, provided that the perlocutionary effect is appropriately chosen. Thus we can put for Strawson's schema the conjunction

A uttered x *and* A, by his utterance of x, meant-nn O

which, in turn, unpacks into

A uttered x *and*

A intended his utterance of x to bring it about that his audience *pick out or identify O* by means of their recognition of that intention.

Approximately this adaptation of the Gricean theory has been made by John R. Searle:

Given that S utters an expression R in the presence of H in a context C then in the literal utterance of R, S successfully and non-defectively performs the speech act of singular identifying reference [to X] if and only if...

5. S intends that the utterance of R will pick out or identify X to H.
6. S intends that the utterance of R will identify X to H by means of H's recognition of S's intention to identify X ...

(*SpA*, 94–5; I have quoted only the operative Gricean clauses.) For the utterance of R to pick out or identify X *to H* is surely for the utterance to bring it about that H picks out or identifies X. Thus Searle's scheme fits the pattern of evocation of perlocutionary effect which we have found characteristically underlying agent-semantics.

Searle offers a similar Gricean unpacking of the linguistic action of *predicating* which joins with referring in Strawsonian agent-semantics to form a full normal act of asserting or stating. I have, however, so far carefully charted my path around predicating and predication, and I intend to continue to do so, for it is my conviction that to engage the issue of linguistic representation in those terms is, already, seriously to distort the logic of that activity. These issues will become clearer as I proceed. For now, I should rather like to take a closer look at Gricean intentions and, in particular, to see what is involved in the adaptation of Grice's view to *designators* used by linguistic agents in acts of referring. 'Means' and, in particular, Grice's 'means-nn' take both claims and designators as objects. Thus, for example, Jones utters the sentence "The most revered living American is a right-winger." One may ask, then, *what* Jones means(-nn) by this utterance of the sentence and, if we give an answer to that question, we shall be giving one as well to the question of *whom* Jones means(-nn) by (his utterance of) the phrase 'the most revered living American'. Thus, if our answer to the question "What does Jones mean?" is

Jones means(-nn) that the evangelist Billy Graham is politically conservative, then our answer to the question "*Whom* does Jones mean?" will be

Jones means(-nn) (by 'the most revered living American') the evangelist Billy Graham (rather than, say, the comedian Bob Hope).

As Grice and Searle unpack it, for Jones to mean(-nn) Billy Graham rather than Bob Hope by his utterance of 'the most revered living American' is for Jones to intend that his audience pick out or identify Billy Graham (by means of their recognition of that intention) and not to intend that they pick out or identify Bob Hope. But in virtue of what is it *Billy Graham* that Jones intends his audience to pick out? What, in other words, needs to be true of *Jones* in order that it be Billy Graham, and not Bob Hope, that he intends his audience to pick out?

These questions have not, of course, gone unnoticed, and Searle raises them explicitly:

> For what is it to *mean* or *intend* a particular object to the exclusion of all others? Some facts incline us to think that it is a movement of the soul – but can I intend just one particular object independent of any description or other form of identification I could make of it? And, if so, what makes my intention an intention directed at just *that* object and not at some other? (*SpA*, 87)

His solution is to fall back upon the notion of an *identifying description.* Identifying descriptions are expressions of certain sorts:

> ... demonstrative presentations, e.g., "that – over there", and descriptions in purely general terms which are true of the object uniquely, e.g., "the first man to run a mile in under 3 minutes, 53 seconds." Both the pure demonstrative and the pure description are limiting cases; and in practice most identifications rely on a mixture of demonstrative devices and descriptive predicates, e.g., "the man *we* saw *yesterday*", or on some other form of secondary referent, which in turn the speaker must be able to identify, e.g., "the author of *Waverley*", "the capital of *Denmark*". ... But these kinds of identifying expressions – demonstrative presentation, unique description, mixed demonstrative and descriptive identification – exhaust the field. (*SpA*, 86)

For a person S to intend his utterance of R to pick out or identify an object X to a hearer H, then, Searle imposes an additional requirement: that

> ... either R contains an identifying description of X or S is able to supplement R with an identifying description of X. (*SpA*, 95)

This he calls the "Principle of Identification".

Now there are, at this point, several remarks that need to be made. The first of these is that Kripke has recently argued persuasively and in general against adopting a Principle of Identification of the sort which Searle espouses. Kripke is concerned with theories of referring which hold that

(1) To every name or designating expression 'X', there corresponds a cluster of properties, namely the family of properties φ such that A believes 'φX'.

(2) One of the properties, or some conjointly, are believed by A to pick out some individual uniquely.

and

(3) If most, or a weighted most, of the φ's are satisfied by one unique object y, then y is the referent of 'X'.

(*NN*, 280) Now Searle's account of referring can be construed as a view answering to this description with only minor modifications. All we need do is to replace "every name or designating expression 'X' " in (1) by "every *use* of a name or designating expression 'X' " and take the conclusion of (3) to

be "then *y* is *A's intended* referent of 'X'." For Searle explicitly holds that
the speaker, A, intends or means by his utterance of 'X' the object *y* by
virtue of the fact that A possesses (in some sense of 'possess' yet to be explored) a uniquely individuating (demonstrative or general) description of *y*
which A associates (in some sense of 'associate' yet to be explored) with his
use of the expression 'X'. We can, in other words, construe Kripke's
criticisms even more broadly – not merely as a critique of "Descriptionist"
theories of *referring*, but as a critique of Descriptionist theories of *intending*
(having in mind) as well. Now Kripke's critique of theories of reference in
the Descriptionist style is extensive, but the following passages are directly
apposite:

> Suppose most of the φ's are in fact satisfied by a unique object. Is that object neces-
> sarily the referent of 'X' for A? Let's suppose someone says that Gödel is the man who
> proved the incompleteness of arithmetic, and this man is suitably well educated and is
> even able to give an independent account of the incompleteness theorem. He doesn't
> just say, 'Well, that's Gödel's theorem', or whatever. He actually states a certain
> theorem which he attributes to Gödel as the discoverer. Is it the case, then, that if most
> of the φ's are satisfied by a unique object *y* then *y* is the referent of the name 'X' for
> A? Let's take a simple case. ... Does it follow that whoever discovered the incom-
> pleteness of arithmetic is the referent of 'Gödel'?
>   Imagine the following blatantly fictional situation. ... Suppose that Gödel was not in
> fact the author of this theorem. A man named 'Schmidt', whose body was found in
> Vienna under mysterious circumstances many years ago, actually did the work in ques-
> tion. His friend Gödel somehow got hold of the manuscript and it was thereafter
> attributed to Gödel. On the view in question, then, when our ordinary man uses the
> name 'Gödel', he really means to refer to Schmidt, because Schmidt is the unique
> person satisfying the description. ... So, since the man who discovered the incom-
> pleteness of arithmetic is in fact Schmidt, we, when we talk about 'Gödel', are in fact
> always referring to Schmidt. But it seems to me that we are not. We simply are not.
> (*NN*, 293–4)

And surely Kripke is correct in this. That the speaker possesses a uniquely
individuating description which he associates with his use of a referring expression simply does not guarantee that the object to which the description
in fact uniquely applies is the object to which the speaker intends to refer
(i.e., which he intends his audience to pick out or identify). The condition
proposed by the Principle of Identification is not sufficient to determine the
object which the speaker intends. Nor is it necessary.

Consider Richard Feynman, to whom many of us are able to refer. He is a leading
contemporary theoretical physicist. Everyone *here* (I'm sure!), can state the contents
of one of Feynman's theories so as to differentiate him from Gell-Mann. However, the
man in the street, not possessing these abilities, may still use the name 'Feynman'.
When asked he will say: well he's a physicist or something. He may not think that this
picks out anyone uniquely. I still think he uses the name 'Feynman' as a name for
Feynman. (*NN*, 292)

And surely this is correct as well. The speaker need not even believe himself to be in possession of a description which uniquely individuates the object to which he intends to refer.[1]

The Principle of Identification, or something quite like it, is operative in Strawson's thought as well. As he views the matter, the paradigm of successful hearer identification is the case in which

... the hearer can pick out by sight or hearing or touch, or can otherwise sensibly discriminate, the particular being referred to, knowing that it is that particular. (*I*, 18)

Strawson speaks of cases of this sort as cases of *demonstrative identification*. Demonstrative identification is, however, notoriously not always possible, and so, in situations of communication, one is constantly forced back upon linguistic means of securing the perlocutionary effect of successful hearer identification. But Strawson, unlike Searle, is not sanguine about the availability of descriptions which, in Searle's terms, "are true of the object uniquely". There is a theoretical worry which Strawson believes must first be laid to rest, for it is arguable that

... however extensive the speaker's knowledge and however extensive the hearer's, neither can know that the former's identifying description in fact applies uniquely. (*I*, 20)

To meet this worry, Strawson claims, "it is sufficient to show how the situation of non-demonstrative identification may be linked with the situation of demonstrative identification." (*I*, 21)

Is it plausible to suppose... that of every particular we may refer to there is some description uniquely relating it to the participants in, or the immediate setting of, the conversation in which the reference is made? ... The universe might be repetitive in various ways. But this fact is no obstacle in principle to supplying descriptions of the kind required. For by demonstrative identification we can determine a common reference point and common axes of spatial direction; and with these at our disposal we have also the theoretical possibility of a description of every other particular in space and time as uniquely related to our reference point. Perhaps not all particulars are in both time *and* space. But it is at least plausible to assume that every particular which is not, is uniquely related in some other way to one which is. (*I*, 22–3)

For Strawson, as we know, these observations give rise to an ontological hierarchy of particulars arranged in order of identifiability dependence — spatio-temporal particulars (material objects and persons) being primary in the order of identification and, thus, ontologically basic, while various "dependent particulars" (events, mental states, etc.) are identifiable by their relations to these basic particulars and, consequently, ontologically secondary as well. I shall have something to say about this project of grounding an ontological system by a consideration of the problems of speaker-hearer identification, but it is not my main concern here.

Strawson's proposal – that all identifying reference be grounded or, at least, groundable ultimately in demonstrative identification – is offered as a solution of the *recognition* problem for reference: how is it possible, in principle, for the hearer to succeed in identifying *that* particular to which the speaker intends to refer, i.e., which the speaker *intends* his audience to pick out or identify? But it suggests, as well, what Strawson's solution must be to the *production* problem for identifying reference: in virtue of what does the speaker intend that it is *that* particular, to the exclusion of others, which his audience is to pick out or identify? Parallel to Searle's Principle of Identification, we should expect to find a Strawsonian principle: that the speaker provide or be able to provide a description of the object of reference uniquely relating that object to others *demonstratively* identifiable there and then by him and by his audience.

Kripke's critique of Descriptionist solutions to the problems of reference applies, of course, equally to Strawson's proposal. There is no reason to suppose – indeed, there are good reasons not to suppose – that any speaker possesses a description of his intended object of reference which uniquely individuates it by relating it spatio-temporally to particulars demonstratively identifiable by him and his audience on the occasion of language-use. But, in addition, we may raise some difficulties concerning the notion of *demonstrative* identification which forms the keystone of Strawson's proposal. In a situation of demonstrative identification, Strawson writes,

an expression is used which, given the setting and accompaniments of its use, can properly, or at least naturally, be taken, as then used, to apply only to a certain single member of the range of particulars which the hearer is able, or a moment before was able, sensibly to discriminate, and to nothing outside that range. Cases of this kind are the cases, *par excellence*, for the use of demonstratives, whether helped out by descriptive words or not... (*I*, 19)

What one should contrast with this passage from Strawson are certain well-known remarks by Wittgenstein (*PI*, #28):

Now one can ostensively define a proper name, the name of a colour, the name of a material, a numeral, the name of a point of the compass, and so on. The definition of the number two, "That is called 'two' " – pointing to two nuts – is perfectly exact. – But how can two be defined like that? The person one gives the definition to doesn't know what one wants to call "two"; he will suppose that "two" is the name given to *this* group of nuts! – He *may* suppose this; but perhaps he does not. He might make the opposite mistake; when I want to assign a name to this group of nuts, he might understand it as a numeral. And he might equally well take the name of a person, of which I give an ostensive definition, as that of a colour, of a race, or even of a point of the compass. That is to say: an ostensive definition can be variously interpreted in *every* case.

Wittgenstein, of course, is not here addressing the precise problem which Strawson proposes to solve. But the view which Wittgenstein *is* discussing bears an important similarity to Strawson's. Strawson would ground all identifying reference in demonstrative identification. The view which Wittgenstein is considering, analogously, is a view which seeks to ground all word-meaning in ostensive definition. One learns the meaning of a word, on this account, in the first instance by hearing the word used in a speech-situation in which the hearer can there and then discriminate the intended "target", as it were, of the word's use – thus, the person referred to, if the word is a proper name used referentially; the color picked out, if the word is a predicate color-adjective used attributively; and so on. Strawson's solution to the problem of identifying reference is an instance of this *general* scheme. One identifies the *referent* of a word, in the first instance, by hearing the word used in a speech-situation in which the hearer can there and then discriminate the intended "target" of the word's use. Again, we see, Strawson's proposal takes the form of a solution to the *recognition* problem for identifying reference. As such, it is open to the Wittgensteinian critique. The theoretical problem which Strawson introduces his reductions to demonstrative identifications to solve is, recall, that

... however extensive the speaker's knowledge and however extensive the hearer's, neither can know that the former's identifying description in fact applies uniquely. (*I*, 20)

Now, on one reading, this is clearly false, for there are many descriptions which, *as a matter of logic* can be known by speaker and hearer to apply uniquely: 'the first dog born at sea', 'the most revered living American', 'the hungriest sheep ever to crop a meadow', and so on. The problem is not, then, as Strawson intimates, that of the speaker and hearer coming to *know that* the speaker's identifying description applies uniquely. The problem is rather that of the speaker and hearer coming to share an understanding of *what it is* to which the identifying description uniquely applies. What is wanted is not that the speaker's description should uniquely specify a particular. *That* requirement is easy to satisfy. What is wanted is rather that the hearer should pick out or identify *the same* particular which the speaker *takes* his description uniquely to specify.

What Wittgenstein's critique of ostensive definition shows us is that a regression to demonstrative identification provides no further guarantee that this requirement is met. For, just as any ostensive definition can be variously interpreted in every case, so *any* demonstrative identification can be variously interpreted in *every* case. The there-and-then discrimin*ability* by

the hearer of the speaker's intended object of reference provides no
assurance that the hearer will *take* that object to be the speaker's intended
referent. For he may take the speaker to be referring to some discriminable
part or quality of that particular or to some complex object having that
particular as a part. It may, indeed, be true that identifying description in
general can be no more secure than demonstrative identification. But this
fact should not lead us to conclude that demonstrative identification can be
more secure than it in fact is. If a demonstrative identification succeeds,
then, it is in large measure because the hearer has already *mastered* the
linguistic apparatus of identifying reference. Demonstrative identification
can no more provide an incorrigible *foundation* for identifying reference in
general than ostensive definition for word-meaning in general. And, if the
hearer and speaker in fact share mastery of the *linguistic* apparatus of
identifying reference, then the use of an identifying description – or even of
a proper name – may succeed in conveying *by itself* all that needs to be
conveyed.

But it is at last time to face squarely the problem which I have been continuing to defer. It can be most sharply highlighted by noting that
Strawson's proposal is *essentially* a solution to the recognition problem. The
recognition problem is a *hearer's* problem. But there is, as I have several
times noted, a parallel *speaker's* problem as well. How does a speaker *intend*
or *mean* one object of reference to the exclusion of all others? I have
spoken of a speaker's "possessing" a description, uniquely individuating or
not, which he "associates" with a particular object. But it is now time to go
into these phrases. My examination of Kripke's critique of Descriptionist
theories of reference highlighted the fact that the intended object of
reference need not be, and frequently, perhaps, is not, that object if any
which the description in question uniquely fits. For, even if "possessing" a
uniquely individuating description, the speaker may take the description to
fit some other object – for example, may *take* the description 'the first dog
born at sea' to fit Rover, even though it is Fido whom the description *in
fact* fits. But what is it for the speaker to *take* his description to fit Rover
rather than Fido? More generally, what is it for a speaker to *take* any description to fit one particular rather than another? It is precisely this question which Wittgenstein is worrying in the following passages:

I remember having meant *him*. Am I remembering a process or state? –When did it
begin, what was its course; etc.? (*PI*, #661)

If I say "I meant *him*" very likely a picture comes to my mind, perhaps of how I
looked at him, etc.; but the picture is only like an illustration to a story. From it alone

it would mostly be impossible to conclude anything at all; only when one knows the story does one know the significance of the picture. (*PI*, #663)

Imagine that you were in pain and were simultaneously hearing a nearby piano being tuned. You say, "It'll soon stop." It certainly makes quite a difference whether you mean the pain or the piano-tuning! – Of course; but what does this difference consist in? ... (*PI*, #666)

. . . For one would naturally like to say: when he meant him, he aimed at him. But how is anyone doing that, when he calls someone else's face to mind?
I mean, how does he call HIM to mind?
How does he call him? (*PI*, #691)

Descriptionist theories will not help us here, for the problem I am *now* addressing is one which is *internal* to such theories. Since the success of identifying reference requires that the hearer should pick out or identify the same particular which the speaker *takes* his description uniquely to specify (for, in the case of a putatively *identifying* reference, the speaker is not using a descriptive phrase D with the sense of "whoever or whatever answers to D"), the question can arise, *however* uniquely individuating the proffered description may – as a matter of logic – be: Does the speaker intend the hearer to pick out that object which the description *in fact* fits? And if the speaker *takes* the description in question to fit some object *other* than that which it in fact fits, the answer to this question will be negative.[2] The particular which the speaker means, or intends, or, generically, *has in mind* may well be different from the particular, if any, which his description (if he "possesses" one at all) uniquely specifies.

While these observations show the explanatory utility of Descriptionism to be, at best, severely limited, we are, in fact, in the position to isolate an even more fundamental failing of Descriptionist views in general. Both Searle and Strawson attempt to channel *intended reference* through uniquely individuating *descriptions*. But for this gambit to have even initial plausibility, it is necessary to suppose – speaking somewhat contentiously – that one is somehow *better off* with respect to the intending of *properties* than with respect to the intending of *particulars*. Yet this presumption is false. The "having in mind" of properties is neither more *nor less* problematic than the "having in mind" of particulars.

For suppose that what I intend is that my audience pick out a cerise octagonal table. The description which I "possess", then, must include the specification 'cerise octagonal table'. It follows that I must be intending, be thinking of, or, more generally, *have in mind* the properties of being cerise, being octagonal, and being a table. This is still a contentious way of speaking, of course, but there *is* a difference which needs to be captured between thinking of a cerise octagonal table and, for example, thinking of a mauve hexagonal desk. In virtue of what do I have in mind something cerise, and not mauve; something octagonal, and not hexagonal; and a table, rather than a desk?

Whether or not Descriptionism provides a solution to the problem of intended reference to *particulars*, it is clear enough that it *cannot* provide an answer to these questions. For if, *per impossible*, I were to have in mind something cerise by virtue of "possessing" a uniquely individuating description of the color cerise (and what would *that* look like?), this would provide, at most, only the next of an infinite series of descriptions, for I should now have to intend (have in mind) each of the individuating properties of cerise appealed to in this latest description in order that it be *cerise* which I intend my description to pick out. And once this is recognized, the strategy of shifting the burden of "intending" from *designated* particulars to *described* particulars is seen for what it is – a displacement of the original question rather than an answer to it.

And so I have arrived at a question which undercuts *all* versions of agent-semantics, however elaborate: What is it for a person to have a certain object – to the exclusion of others – in mind? And this is Wittgenstein's question as well.

Now to this question there are, as I see it, only two possible answers. The first of these is ontological. It views *thinking of* as a unique *relation* between persons and the objects of their thought. The second once again relocates our fundamental question, for it is to view *thinking of* on the model of *speaking of*. In brief, thought is to be construed as just *another* representational system. Let me take up these alternatives in order.

On the first, ontological, account, I am thinking of Billy Graham, and not Bob Hope, if I stand in a particular relation to Billy Graham which I do not, at that time, bear to Bob Hope as well. But what relation? Here we come hard up against the problem of not-being. For I can, evidently, think of objects which do *not* exist as easily as I can think of those which *do* exist. So one may be tempted to call *thinking of* an "extraordinary" relation. But to speak in this way is not to resolve a puzzle; it is only to baptize one. How does this "extraordinary" relation work?

The classical solution is to invest the object-term of the relation with some *mode of being*. Thus one may say that the intended referent has (following Descartes) *objective* (as opposed to *formal*) being, or (following Brentano) that it *intentionally inexists* in the thought, or (following Meinong) that it *subsists*.

After all, the argument has run, thinking of, say, Pegasus is different from thinking of nothing at all. For thinking of Pegasus *is* thinking and thinking of nothing at all is not thinking at all. So thinking of Pegasus is thinking of *something*. And now, the argument continues, if I am thinking of *something*, then there must *be* something of which I am thinking — in *some* sense of 'be'. Not, of course, that there *exists* something of which I am thinking — for Pegasus doesn't exist — but still there *is* something of which I am thinking. And so one is led to posit *modes* of being. This line of argument will be recognized as one of venerable ancestry:

> Socrates: Then is the same sort of thing possible in any other case?
> Theatetus: What sort of thing?
> Socr. That a man should see something, and yet what he sees should be nothing.
> Theat. No. How could that be?
> Socr. Yet surely if what he sees is something, it must be a thing that is. Or do you suppose that 'something' can be reckoned among things that have no being at all?
> Theat. No, I don't.
> Socr. Then, if he sees something, he sees a thing that is.
> Theat. Evidently.
> Socr. And if he hears a thing, he hears something and hears a thing that is.
> Theat. Yes.
> Socr. And if he touches a thing, he touches something, and if something, then a thing that is.
> Theat. That also is true.
> Socr. And if he thinks, he thinks something, doesn't he?
> Theat. Necessarily.
> Socr. And when he thinks something, he thinks a thing that is?
> Theat. I agree.
> Socr. So to think what is not is to think nothing.
> Theat. Clearly.
> Socr. But surely to think nothing is the same as not to think at all.
> Theat. That seems plain.
> Socr. If so, it is impossible to think what is not, either about anything that is, or absolutely.
> (Plato, *T*, 188E–189B)

Plato's version of the argument has the virtue of making explicit the analogy from which it derives whatever initial plausibility it has: an analogy between thinking (conception) and seeing (perception). 'Think of' is assimilated to the model of 'see', 'hear', and 'touch', and these verbs of perception are, in Ryle's sense, achievement words. Merely saying this, however, should suggest a variety of crucial *dis*analogies.

Where there can be success, there can also be failure. Thus we have not only seeing but also *seeming to see*; not only hearing, but also *seeming to hear*. These verbs of *appearing* are designed for just the case in which the presumed target of the putative perceptual act of seeing or hearing does not exist, paradigmatically in instances of hallucination. The case in which I seem to see (but fail actually to see) a pool of water is precisely the case in which my experience is indistinguishable in certain respects from that of actually seeing a pool of water, but in which there exists no pool of water suitably located to be the target of my putative perceptual act. Thus, if *thinking of* were genuinely analogous to seeing, hearing, or, in general, to perceiving, we should expect to find "conceptual hallucinations" parallel to perceptual hallucinations. There are, of course, cases of *failing to think of.* These, however, are not analogues to *seeming* to see, but rather to failing to see because, for example, the (extant) object is too far away or because there are too many trees in the way. Thus I may fail to see a bull not because there exists no bull to be seen but because the bull is hiding behind the fence. For an act of perception, then, there are two ways in which it can go wrong: non-existence of the putative object of perception (where, however, some act substantively analogous to one of veridical perception – viz. hallucination – *is* brought off) and failure, resulting from *adverse conditions*, to perceive an extant object. Verbs of perception in general go with clusters of limiting conditions, and, in that sense, the second sort of failure to perceive is a limit case. One can see more or less clearly, hear more or less well, and so on.

Thinking of is not like that. If I fail to think of a counter-example, this *may* be because there exists no counter-example to be thought of – but this is not conceptual hallucination. It is not *seeming* to think of a counter-example. What counts as seeming to think of a counter-example is *actually thinking* of something, but something which is not, in fact, a counter-example. What counts as seeming to see a pool of water, however, need not be actually seeing something which is not, in fact, a pool of water. For it may not be *seeing* at all. It may be hallucination. Nor, in addition, are there standard or optimal or limiting conditions for thinking of. And if I fail to think of a counter-example when there exists, in fact, a counter-example to be thought of, it is not because the counter-example is too far away or hiding behind a conceptual fence.

One should resist, then, the attempt to assimilate *thinking of* to the model of ordinary verbs of (veridical) perception. Its logic is really quite different. And that being so, the only plausible support of the idea that thinking is a relation between a person and objects having an extraordinary mode of being is undercut. Not, of course, that the notion of modes of being is entirely problem-free in its own right. As developed in the Cartesian theory of objective being or Brentano's view of intentional inexistence, it is a creaky, old, essentially Scholastic machine which I, at least, have lost the knack of making operate. And once one has undercut the perceptual analogy which lends initial plausibility to the modes-of-being thesis, there is,

I think, no independent ground for trying to get that machine in operation. So I reject this answer to our problem about the directedness of thoughts.

What approach remains then? Look again at Wittgenstein's remark (*PI*, #691):

... For one would naturally like to say: when he meant him he aimed at him. But how is anyone doing that, when he calls someone else's face to mind?

I mean, how does he call HIM to mind?

How does he call him?

I think that the correct way to read this remark is as follows: There is an analogy between calling someone, say Jones, *to mind* and *calling Jones*. And how does one call Jones? One utters his name! The suggestion, then, is that we invert the order of argument which we have been pursuing. Rather than attempting to ground *speaking of* by an appeal to speakers' intentions and, thus, to *thinking of*, the proposal is that we understand *thinking of* by analogy with *speaking of*. I speak of one object to the exclusion of others by employing an expression which *designates* that object, and not others. I speak of Billy Graham and not Bob Hope by using the name 'Billy Graham' and not the name 'Bob Hope'. What I want to suggest is that, similarly, I *think* of Billy Graham, and not Bob Hope, by deploying (in thought) some (covert, psychic) designator of Billy Graham. Briefly: thought is to be construed as a representational system.

This approach is clearly adequate to provide an answer to the question concerning the having in mind of *properties* which proved the sticking point of Descriptionism. If one eschews modes of being and concludes that my thought of a cerise octagonal table does not consist in a relationship between me and a *subsistent* cerise octagonal table (having objective being or intentionally inexistent in my thought), then the only viable course seems to be that I deploy (in some sense) a psychic constituent which bears to cerise objects, for example, that relationship (*whatever* it turns out to be) which the *word* 'cerise' bears to cerise objects; and some psychic constituent which bears to octagonal objects the relationship which the word 'octagonal' bears to octagonal objects; and some psychic constituent which bears to tables the relationship which the word 'table' bears to tables. And this relationship is, loosely speaking, one of "standing for" (denoting, in one classical sense) or, more precisely, it is a relationship of *representing*.

It is important to note that by 'covert designator' or 'psychic constituent', I do *not* mean 'mental image' or 'mental tokening of a public-language word'. In this I am following Wittgenstein's original reply to Russell (*N*, 130):

"Does a Gedanke [thought] consist of words?" No! But of psychical constituents that
have the same sort of relation to reality as words. What those constituents are I don't
know.

To say this is not to say, of course, that mental images fail to occur. They
may indeed occur and may even resemble what they are images of in that
peculiar sense of 'resemble' in which a *mental* image *can* be said to resemble
a physical object. (But see here Dennett, *C&C*, 132–46.) The relation of
representation, however, cannot consist in such a resemblance. Mental
images *could*, indeed, have a role in thought quite like the role of inscriptions in written language or, perhaps a closer analogy, like the role of
paint-patterns-on-canvas in representational depiction. But it is not by virtue
of its resemblance to what it represents that a word (token) "stands for"
what it does, nor is it by virtue of its resemblance to what it represents that
a portrait depicts what it does. On this topic, I shall have much more to say
later.

On the other hand, we must be careful not to overstate the case. In discussing mental imagery, Wittgenstein speaks of the way in which a mental
image is *used.* (See, e.g., *PI,* #73–74.) And I have spoken of "deploying" a
covert designator. We must take great care not to think of these as *illocutionary* uses. When I commune with myself, I do not *communicate* with
myself. The difficulty with theories of the mind's eye is that they lead in-
evitably to theories of the mind's mind. Thought is not a picture-gallery of
the mind. It is not a dialogue within the soul. It is not even a monologue
within the soul. The analogy which I am pressing holds this far and no
farther: That thought shares with representative depiction and with overt
language the feature of *being a system of representations.*

The view of conceptual thought which I have just been sketching is not, of
course, original. Its roots, we have just seen, go at least as far back as the
Tractatus. It has been developed in considerable detail by Wilfrid Sellars
(*EPM, B&BK, SRLG, S&M*) and, independently, by Peter Geach (*MA*), and
has been explored at length by Bruce Aune (*KM&N*). But if it is correct
– and, with the abandonment of modes of being, I see no alternative – it
reveals the ultimate sterility of agent-semantics and its intentionalist underpinnings. For if thought *is* a representational system analogous to public
language, then it cannot be appealed to to *explain* how representational
systems succeed in representing a world. Whatever the merits of agent-
semantics as a component in an account of public linguistic *performances*,
the analysis of *representation* must be conducted at a level undercutting the
distinction between the overt and the covert, between public language and
thought. This, as I read it, is one of the main lessons of the *Philosophical*

Investigations, and it is paradoxical on that account that the *Investigations* has also provided the main incentive for intentionalistically grounded theories of agent-semantics.

Thus, while it is doubtless in some sense *true* to say that bits of language don't represent but, rather, it is people who *use* bits of language to represent, at a more fundamental level it is true that a person can use something overt to represent only by deploying — by backing it with — something covert which represents *in the same sense.* And, on pain of infinite regress, 'deploy' cannot here be parsed as 'use' *in the illocutionary sense.* Of course, actions of people *will* necessarily come into the story of representation. But these will not be *semantic* actions of referring or predicating or stating; nor will they be covert counterparts of semantic actions — agent-semantics shoved indoors. Rather they will need to be *real activities*, considered in extension. And this insight is what brings us to a "form of life", in the most accurate and literal sense.

CHAPTER III

RULES

I want now to return to a theme which I introduced in Chapter I. I there briefly sketched an argument for the view that language is a *rule-governed* system and an argument against the stronger position that language is a *rule-constituted* system. The case for rule-governedness was, briefly, this: that only if we grant that language users have a shared system of rules for making and understanding claims can we understand how diverse speakers' finite linguistic resources can be *uniformly* projected into potentially infinite combinatorial possibilities. The thesis that language is rule-governed, in other words, was offered to account for what I called the creative production competence and the creative recognition competence for claims.

The argument against the thesis that language is a rule-constituted system traded on an analogy of linguistic *mistakes* and violations of the strategic principles, but not the constitutive rules, of such games as chess. I noted, in short, the phenomenon of free deviation from the norm and concluded, on that basis, that if the notion of a rule enters into an account of linguistic representation, it does so in a way different from the way in which it features in accounts of such games as chess. Later I shall want to explore the now-traditional language-chess analogy in more detail. First, however, I should like to examine an argument which cuts not only against the strong view that language is a rule-constituted system but against the more limited thesis that language is a rule-governed system as well.

The argument which I have in mind derives from Ziff, who will have no truck with the notion of a linguistic rule.

I am concerned with regularities: I am not concerned with rules. Rules have virtually nothing to do with speaking or understanding a natural language. . . . An appeal to rules in the course of discussing the regularities to be found in a natural language is as irrelevant as an appeal to the laws of Massachusetts while discussing the laws of motion.

(*SA*, 34–5) The argument consists in the observation that a rule-governed system cannot, as a language can, be learned without being taught.

If there were "rules of language" then, presumably such rules would be laid down in the course of teaching the language. This is another confusion: one is not taught one's native language, one learns it. (*SA*, 35)

Let me develop the point. Learning to behave according to certain rules is, presumably, learning to pursue or eschew certain activities. But it is not simply that. A pigeon who has been trained (conditioned) to peck at a key under certain circumstances has not learned to behave according to any rules. What more is required is that the activities in question be pursued or eschewed *because* they are enjoined or proscribed by the rules. If an agent is *following* a rule in the course of his activities, then, the rule in question must, in some sense, be "present to the mind". This is, of course, a carefully muddy statement. 'In some sense' includes, presumably, such counterfactual senses as "If the agent were appropriately queried...", and 'present to the mind' is left purposely vague for the moment. The point is that what distinguishes a case of an agent's *following* a rule (obeying it) from a case in which his behavior happens to *accord* with it (merely conforming to it) is that, in the former case, a citation of the relevant rule is part of the *explanation* of the agent's behavior. It is his *reason* for behaving (or not behaving) in a certain way. Now a rule which enjoins or proscribes a certain practice must somehow secure reference to that practice. As the practices at issue in putative rules of language are *linguistic* practices, then, in order to secure reference to them, the rules in question must have a *metalinguistic* character. Thus if learning to speak a language consists in learning to follow or obey rules, it seems to presuppose a command, in some sense of 'command', of a metalanguage. As Sellars suggestively puts it:

... it is as though when asked 'How did German words come to be meaningful to Schmidt?' someone were to say, 'Well, before learning German, he knew English – though not to speak out loud – and his compatriots, by a clever combination of gestures and the production of vocables in the presence of objects, brought him to formulate to himself (in English) and obey such rules as "red objects are to be called *rot*". (*SRLG*, 334–5)

This is the Augustinian model of language-learning criticized by Wittgenstein in the early sections of the *Philosophical Investigations*. It is an essentially *inductive* model of language-learning, and Wittgenstein's criticism echoes the suggestion which I have just made:

Someone coming into a strange country will sometimes learn the language of the inhabitants from ostensive definitions that they give him; and he will often have to *guess* the meaning of these definitions; and will guess sometimes right, sometimes wrong.
And now, I think, we can say: Augustine describes the learning of human language as if the child came into a strange country and did not understand the language of the country; that is, as if it already had a language, only not this one. Or again: as if the child could already *think*, only not yet speak. And "think" would here mean something like "talk to itself". (*PI*, #32)

Thus, viewing language as a rule-governed activity (in the sense that language use consists in following or obeying rules) appears to lead to a regress. The acquisition of a language will presuppose the command of a metalanguage (or the covert, intentionalistic, counterpart of such an overt command). And this will not do. The suggested conclusion, then, is that the fact that language is finitely learnable without teaching is incompatible with its being a rule-governed system. Learning a language cannot be a matter of learning to follow or obey rules.

Yet the case *for* rules is compelling as well. Even Ziff recognizes, in addition to linguistic regularities, what he calls *principles* and *projections*. An example of a projection is this: That if 'The cat is on the mat.' is uttered then, in the standard case, some feline is on some mat. Now 'standard' here cannot have reference to the statistical norm, the typical case. For the *regularity* is, as Ziff notes, quite different:

If 'The cat is on the mat.' is uttered then generally a philosophicogrammatical discussion is under way. (*SA*, 60)

The projection in question, then, is not inductively derived from the observable regularity in speech behavior, but rather requires for its justification a certain principle, the principle of composition.

Roughly speaking, it is a principle to the effect that the relevant similarity between distinct semantic correlates of u_i and u_j be a reflection of the relevant similarity between the two utterances. (*SA*, 62)

And Ziff, of course, recognizes the indispensibility of such principles.

To deny the principle of composition would, I am inclined to suppose, be utterly absurd. Either the new utterance is arbitrarily explicated then and there or the explication is at least partially predetermined by the syntactic structure of the utterance. If every new utterance had then and there to be arbitrarily explicated, the corpus of utterances would not even resemble a language. (*SA*, 61–2)

Now the principle of composition is an *observer's* principle, a theoretician's principle. But what we should focus on here is Ziff's notion of "arbitrary explication". Explication is a *hearer's* activity. In fact, the denial of arbitrary explication is precisely the assertion of what I have called the creative recognition competence for claims. Ziff evidently thinks of hearer-understanding as the product of some activity — the activity of explication — and concurs that the possession of a recognition *competence* on the part of hearers constrains the possible forms of such activity. Explication cannot be arbitrary. But what alternative is there to arbitrary explication except explication according to some rule?

Speaking a language is engaging in a (highly complex) rule-governed form of behavior.

To learn and master a language is (*inter alia*) to learn and have mastered these rules. (Searle, *SpA*, 12)

This is the conclusion which seems to be dictated by the facts of creative production and recognition competence, much as the opposite conclusion appeared to be dictated by the facts of finite learnability without teaching. And so we have a dilemma. I think it is a resolvable dilemma, but, in order to resolve it, we shall first need to assemble some preliminary considerations. One way to begin is by raising some questions about the notion of a rule of language in general.

If there are rules of language, what do they look like? This is a question which has been little faced in the literature, but Aaron Snyder has provided us with a list of possible candidates:

The following might be advanced as rules of the English language:
Of spelling:
  1. 'I' before 'e' except after 'c'.
  2. In forming a regular ("-ed") past tense, the final consonant is doubled only if the last syllable is accented.
Of punctuation:
  3. The first word of a sentence must begin with a capital letter.
  4. Foreign expressions not yet assimilated into English are italicized.
Of grammar:
  5. When 'lie' means "recline", the past tense is 'lay'.
  6. 'I' is the first person singular pronoun in the nominative.
Of meaning:
  7. 'Infer' means "draw a consequence", not "suggest a consequence".
  8. 'Euphoric' means "happy, buoyant, having a sense of extreme well-being; high".
Of use:
  9. 'Hello' is used as a term of informal greeting.
  10. 'Sir' may only be used in addressing males.
And perhaps such things as:
  11. Pronouns must have a clear referent in the discursive context.
  12. Commands may only be given by persons in a position of authority relative to those persons to whom the command is given. (*RL*, 165)

Now what I want to suggest is particularly striking about these examples is how *little* some of them look like rules. In particular, (7) and (8) — which are clearly of central concern, given our interest in language as a system of representation — resist *any* natural formulation in normative or imperative language. What does a rule look like? The key point is that a rule is a rule for *doing something*. Rules connect essentially with actions, activities, behavior. *Prima facie*, they can connect in three ways. A rule may be prescriptive; it may specify that some action is to be done, must be done, or ought to be done. Or a rule may be prohibitive (proscriptive); it may specify that some action is not to be done, may or must not be done, or ought not be done. Or a rule may be permissive; it may specify that some action may be done or is permitted or allowed. But what actions, activities, or behavior are at issue in rules of *language*?

Well, for some of Snyder's examples, appropriate behavior is not too difficult to isolate. (1) through (4), (9), (10), and (12), for example, give no particular trouble in this regard. But it is interesting to note that the closer Snyder's examples come to making contact with the function of language as a system of representation, the more resistant his examples become to normative formulations. In the key cases of (7) and (8), in fact, the only actions we find available are precisely the actions I earlier bracketed under the rubric "agent-semantics". (7), for example, reformulates in the imperative only as:

(7i) Use 'infer' to mean 'draw a consequence', not 'suggest a consequence' and analogously for (8). Now in Chapter II I explored in detail the sterility of agent-semantics. Such actions as 'using... to mean —', while they are doubtless performed by persons on many occasions, cannot be terms of the *analysis* of language as a system of representation which we are seeking, for they logically presuppose it. In addition, however, (7i) brings us squarely up against the Ziff-Sellars-Wittgenstein criticism of rule-governedness which I outlined above. For (7i) is a rule in the metalanguage which can only be *followed* by someone who *already* knows what 'draw a consequence' and 'suggest a consequence' mean, and thus, if knowing what a term means is knowing the rules for *its* use, already knows some other rules of language. And, if language is to be learnable, at least not *all* rules of language can be of this sort.

If there are rules of language, there must be some behavior or activity which they regulate. What activity is this? What I wish to suggest is that the relevant activity is *inference*. Rules of language, in the appropriate sense, regulate the activity of *drawing consequences*. They are rules of inference.

On the face of it, this is an implausible suggestion, but I hope to make it more plausible as we proceed. In any case, that there *are* rules of inference should not be open to any serious dispute. The clinching argument, I should think, was provided by Lewis Carroll in "What the Tortoise Said to Achilles". His argument there concerned, in particular, a formal rule — *modus ponens* — and what Carroll demonstrated was that, on pain of infinite regress, the *rule* of *modus ponens* could not be replaced in reasoning by its corresponding conditional. What may not be so clear is that there are *non-formal* rules of inference, or, as I shall call them, *content rules*, of correspondingly non-derivative authority: rules in which the non-logical (descriptive) terms occur essentially (rather than vacuously). But there is a way in which this, too, can be argued, at least for a broad class of languages.

If one holds that all rules of inference of non-derivative authority are *formal* rules, then one is constrained to view the argument:

(1)   Albany is west of Boston
Therefore ────────────────────────────
(2)   Boston is east of Albany

as an *enthymeme*, for no formal rule of inference will license the conclusion of (2) from the single premiss (1). There will be, then, a "suppressed premiss", presumably something like:

(3)   If Albany is west of Boston, then Boston is east of Albany

which allows one to derive (2) by an application of *modus ponens*, a formal rule. And, if we inquire into the sources of (3), we are likely to be led to an argument of the following sort as the full-dress form of the original putative enthymeme:

(1)   Albany is west of Boston   Given
(4)   (x) (y) (If x is west of y, then y is east of
           x)
(3)   If Albany is west of Boston, then Boston   From (4) by UI
           is east of Albany   twice
Therefore,_____

(2)   Boston is east of Albany.

This, however, simply delays the moment of reckoning, for what justification are we going to put opposite (4) in the argument? It is, presumably, a premiss. But where does it come from?

Well, at this point one is likely to be told a variety of things. (4), it may be said, is *analytic*; it is true by virtue of the meanings of the terms 'east' and 'west'. I'm inclined, in fact, to think that this is correct, although no argument is needed nowadays to establish that the notion of analyticity or truth *ex vi terminorum* is problem-ridden. I shall have more to say on this topic later. The point to be made now, however, is that *this* answer — true, false, or empty — is unhelpful. Until we have a better idea of what to make of "meaning", an appeal to that notion explains or clarifies nothing.

The question which I should like to press is that of how we are to interpret the 'if...then...' of (4). It is part and parcel of my argument here that 'if...then...' *needs* interpreting. Specifically, I want to argue that the conditional in (4) cannot be interpreted as the *material* conditional of standard logic without loss of strength. For, *whatever* its backing, (4) is surely strong enough to support *counterfactual* inferences. That is, whatever authorizes (4) licenses the inference not only of (3) but also of

> (3.1)   If Boston *were* west of Albany, then Albany *would be* east of Boston.

'If...then...' is, in other words, ambiguous. We can disambiguate it by adding appropriate riders to (4). If we do so, then, we get the following two readings:

> (4.1)   (x) (y) (If x is west of y, then, *in fact*, y is east of x)

> (4.2)   (x) (y) (If x is west of y, then, *necessarily*, y is east of x).

The truth of such synthetic counterfactuals as (3.1), I want to hold, demands that we read (4) as (4.2) rather than (4.1).

Now it is not immediately clear that we are any better off. We have traded the problem of analyticity for the problem of interpreting the adverb 'necessarily' in its application to a conditional, a trick which people have surely known how to perform since Quine's "Two Dogmas of Empiricism". We have, in fact, stumbled across a *family* of locutions and constructions for which we need an account. I have already marked the subjunctive mood as deployed in counterfactual reasoning and assertion. This led, in turn, to 'necessarily', 'but 'necessarily' is only one of a variety of locutions used to mark a phenomenon which still stands in need of explication. This family includes the use of 'can't' in

If the ball is uniformly red, then it *can't* be green as well
and that of 'must' in

If the patch is red then it *must* be colored, and, since it is colored, it *must* have a shape.

I want to interpret all of these locutions and constructions — I shall call them 'terms of semantic appraisal' — as the *object language markers of content rules of inference.* Thus, the backing of (4) is *indicated* by (4.2) to be the rule of inference

> (4*)   (x) (y) (*that* x is west of y *implies that* y is east of x).

Implication I take to be the converse of inferability. To say that

> that p *implies* that q

is just to say that

that q *may be inferred from* that p,

and here I finally make contact with the discussion of rules which I initiated earlier, for the form

φ may be inferred from ψ

is the schema of a permissive rule, authorizing a performance. My thesis, in short, is that what *ultimately* licenses the introduction of (3) into the original argument is the content rule:

(4**)   (x)(y)(that y is east of x may be inferred from that x is west of y).

But this rule authorizes the inference from (1) to (2) *non-enthymematically.*

Let me review the course of the reasoning. In order to construe the argument from (1) to (2) as enthymematic, it was necessary to provide a suppressed premiss, (3). That premiss, in turn, stood in need of justification, and we were led to see it as an instance of a general conditional truth, (4), in which the words 'west' and 'east' occurred essentially. The force of that general conditional, I argued, was such as to not be appropriately captured by reading the 'if...then...' which it contained as a material conditional. It had the sense of (4.2) rather than (4.1). At this point, we have a choice. 'Necessarily' in (4.2) signaled the unconditional assertibility of (4) as a step in formal reasoning. I proposed, instead, that we look upon (4) as the counterpart conditional of a content rule of inference, (4**). *The key point is that this amounts to the same thing.* It is not that the thesis that all inference is formal is one to which we cannot consistently adhere. We can, of course; but there is a price for such adherence. The price is the recognition of unconditionally assertible general conditional truths – analytic truths, if you will – and that price is *equivalent* to the recognition of content rules of non-derivative authority which authorize the original inference from (1) to (2) directly and non-enthymematically.[1] And *since* these prices are equivalent, there is no reason to insist on the thesis that all inference is formal inference. But there is, I think, some reason to pay the price in its inferential rather than its conditional form. One reason I have already suggested: By adverting to content rules of inference, we make contact with the language of action. For inference is performance; drawing a conclusion is something a person *does.* And in our search for a sense in which language use could be a rule-governed activity, we were initially blocked by our failure to locate activities and behaviors outside the closed circle of agent-semantics which could appropriately be enjoined, proscribed, or permitted by the putative linguistic rules. What *kind* of performance inference is remains, of course, to be explored, for it may not yet be clear that we *are* free of agent-semantics. But the line of reasoning which led to the notion of a content rule is, at least, not obviously sterile, as intentionalistic agent-semantics turned out to be.

There is, I think, a second, deeper, reason for paying the price in terms of content rules rather than unconditionally assertible general conditionals, but that will have to emerge as I proceed. For now, I shall simply take it that there *are* content rules of inference and proceed to work out some of the implications of that recognition.

It has been fashionable for some time to construe language and language-use on an analogy with games — typically chess — and game-playing. What has not been equally fashionable, unfortunately, is a detailed exploration of the respects in which language and games are supposed to be analogous. In consequence, I believe, three themes have gotten tangled up in a single analogy, and I should like to take the time now to disentangle them.

The first theme is that of what I shall call a *pure normative characteriza-tion*. This is what is at issue in discussions which stress the fact that chess can be played with a variety of different sorts of "pieces". Sellars provides an articulate example:

> What is it to come to see that two games of independent origin are different ways of playing one and the same game? Surely it is in the first instance to see that a common game vocabulary could be introduced and associated with generic empirical criteria of which the two sets of criteria for the two game vocabularies would be determinate forms. To see this *from outside*, as it were, is to see that they could be regarded as different ways of playing one and the same game. To put such an embracing game vocabulary to actual use is to see them *from inside* as different ways of playing the same game.
>
> Thus, if Texans had independently developed a game played with automobiles and counties called "Tess," with its own distinctive vocabulary for its pieces and moves, we might have come *first* to appreciate isolated similarities between Tess and chess, and *then* to see that they could (along the above lines) be regarded as different ways of playing a [single] game... At this stage, instead of coining a new vocabulary for the "same game," we would probably raise the criteria for being a "pawn," a "king," a "board," and consequently for being a game of chess, to a higher degree of abstraction, and begin to contrast "Texas chess" with "conventional chess" as (materially) different varieties of chess. ...Only after this step could we speak, without qualification, of two forms of the same game. (*AE*, 239—9)

Sellars speaks here of "raising the criteria for being a 'pawn'... to a higher degree of abstraction". He envisions the splitting of the criteria for being a piece of a certain kind, in general, into an (accidental) descriptive and an (essential) prescriptive component, and of coming to use such game-terms as 'pawn' in such a way that their criteria of application are *purely* prescriptive.

Thus, if... the moves of a game are specified in relatively generic terms, the potentiality exists for a similar distinction between the moves as specified in terms of permissions relating to these generically characterized alterations of the *status quo*, and the various recognized "materializations" of the move. The latter would usually go hand in hand with the specification of what were to count as the different kinds of pieces and, if one is necessary, what was to count as the board.

Since the empirical criteria for pieces, positions and moves are always, of necessity, to some degree generic, the potentiality for a distinction between these pieces, positions, and moves, and a plurality of recognized "embodiments" of them in empirically different "materials" and, hence, of different "materializations" *of the same game* is always present. (*AE*, 237)

The notion of a pawn or, more generally, of a piece and of the game in which it is a piece, is here given what I call a pure normative characterization. A pawn is thought of as a something (it doesn't matter what) which moves and captures according to certain rules. Not, of course, that there are *no* material constraints. Pawns must be recognizable as such and, thus, recognizably different from, say, bishops, but it is not criterial for something's being a pawn that it be round-knobbed atop or manufactured in Bavaria. 'Pawn', we may say, is a *normative kind*.

This notion is akin to that of a *functional kind*. What is criterial for an object's being, say, a can-opener is that it have a certain function – that it be *for* opening cans. This is not to say that it need be *used* for opening cans, for a heavy electric can-opener makes an excellent doorstop and may be so used. Opening cans, however, must be its purpose, its *intended* or *characteristic* use. This I leave purposely vague. What is important is the way in which it contrasts with the notion of a structural kind. To qualify as a can-opener, there is nothing in particular that an object must look like or be composed of. Not, of course, that it can be made of just anything. Its structure must be *adequate* to its function and, thus, there are (derivative) structural *constraints*. One cannot make a can-opener entirely of foam rubber, for such a thing *could not* open cans. But the notion of a can-opener is not like that of, say, a marble sphere. An object must have a certain shape and be composed of a specific material to qualify as an instance of *that* kind. Bronze spheres will not do, nor will marble ellipsoids.[2]

Normative kinds are like functional kinds. Empirical objects qualify as members of normative kinds by being caught up in human activities conducted according to rules. An object will be a piece of a certain normative kind by virtue of its being correctly positioned and moved according to a way specified by the rules. And the rules may specify, too, what counts as a position or as a move. "Chess piece" is a normative kind, and *one* point of the analogy between language and games is to suggest that, like chess pieces, bits of language are also essentially members of *normative* kinds. But *what* bits of language?

Let me, for now at least, take it that it is *claims*. In Chapter I, I argued that speaking of sentences and speaking of claims were two modes of talk about what is, ontologically, one subject matter – natural linguistic objects. I can now say somewhat more precisely what these two modes of talk are. The sentence-mode is structural talk; and the claim-mode is pure normative characterizing talk. To say of a sentence that it is a particular claim – e.g., the claim that Albany is west of Boston – is thus analogous to saying of a bit of white plastic standing on the colored cardboard in front of you that it is a pawn. It is to characterize what is, ontologically, an inscription – an array of atoms, if you will – as belonging to a pure normative kind. That kind is wholly constituted by a set of rules – the relevant content rules of inference.

To see this, however, I must develop the second theme tangled up in the language-chess analogy. If using language is analogous to playing chess, what counts as a *piece*, what counts as a *position*, and what counts as a *move*? The traditional way of interpreting the analogy has been to take *bits of language* as the pieces. A move, on this view, would be the *using* of one of these bits – an utterance. Thus, for example, claims have been viewed on analogy with pieces and making a claim (claiming) on analogy with moving a piece. All this, I believe, is radically mistaken. A claim is analogous to a *piece* only in having purely normative identity conditions.

On the view which I have been developing, moves are not utterances but *inferences*. A claim, then, will not be the analogue of a piece but rather of a *position*. What, then, are the pieces? There is only one. What moves from position to position is the language *user*. In this language game, the player is the only piece. Inference (the move) takes the player (piece) from one claim (position) to another claim (position). 'Position' here has a certain ambiguity, as it does in chess. In chess, we speak of *the* position of the pieces at a certain time, and this will be determined by the positions of the pieces at that time. So we have a distributive sense of 'position' in which *each* piece has *a* position at a time and a collective sense of 'position' in which the complete arrangement of all the pieces on the board at a time counts as *the* position of the pieces at that time. A single claim is, on the analogy which I am developing, a position in the *distributive* sense. But there is also a player-piece's position in the collective sense. In this language game, unlike chess, the piece can "occupy" many (distributive) positions simultaneously. As a first approximation, then, take the (collective) position at a time to be constituted by *all* the claims "actively accepted" by a language-user at that time, i.e., by all the (distributive) positions which he occupies at that time. Again, unlike chess, the piece may move (occupy a *new* distributive position) in this language game without abandoning any of its *former* distributive positions. It does, of course, abandon its former collective position – in this case, however, by enriching it.

I am proposing, then, that we view claims as analogous to *positions* on a chessboard. It should be clear that, just as 'chess piece' admits of a pure normative characterization, 'position' also admits of a pure normative characterization. What is essential to the identification of a square on a chessboard *as such* (e.g., as 3rd rank, 2nd file) is that it bear certain relations of orthogonality and adjacency to other positions which, in turn, bear certain relations of adjacency and orthogonality to yet others. And what counts as "adjacency" and "orthogonality" may differ from one material embodiment of the game to another – cashing out, in one instance for example, as the difference between '101100' and '101101' in the memory bank of some chess-playing computer; in another, as the sharing of a county-line in Texas. Similarly, what is essential to the identification of a claim *as such* is its immediate inferential relationships (via content rules) to other claims which, in turn, bear certain immediate inferential relationships to yet other claims, and so on.

This inference-constituted game-board, however, must not be confused with yet a third theme drawn from the chess analogy. In chess, there is an *initial* position. Have we anything like that for language? Well, just as the language-user *qua* piece can occupy many distributive positions (accept many claims) simultaneously, he can also have a variety of *entrances* to the network of inferentially-related positions. Inferences can be drawn from false claims as readily as from true ones. Crucial to our concern with language, however, is its ability to represent the non-linguistic world correctly or accurately. If, crudely, we take the language-user's collective position at a time to be a synchronic cross-section of his evolving representation of the world, we may look upon his activities as moves in a *truth*-game, entered by variously responding to non-linguistic (perceptual) stimuli with the occupying of a linguistic position. Entry to the inferential network, on this view, is not, however, a move *in* the game – much as setting up a board is not a move *in* chess. And the moves in the game are now thought of as conducted with a certain end-in-view, the end of evolving a *complete and accurate* representation of the world (representational checkmate).[3]

Linguistic responses to non-linguistic stimuli are, to be sure, also learned. Thus any particular *initial* perceptual response is subject to revision if its inferential development *within* the network of positions thus entered brings one up against an already accepted claim (occupied position) with which it conflicts. In a sense, then, the collective position of a player-piece in the truth-game is undergoing continual shaping by the world. The constraints on this process are precisely the subject matter of epistemology, and I shall have much more to say about them in succeeding chapters. What is important now is that, on the view which I am developing, truth will be primarily a matter of the adjustment of the *collective* position of the player to the world. Each *distributive* position (claim), however, derives its (normative) identity not through its *empirical* relationships to the world but through its *inferential* relationships to other claims, true *or* false.[4] Now one nice thing to mean by the "meaning" of a linguistic item is its relative location within the inferential network. That is, one nice way to interpret statements of synonymy is as locating two bits of language (or bits of two languages) in the same relative position within the normatively characterized inferential network of claims. Synonymy, on this construal, is substitutability *salve* inference potential. If this is so, however, it will be to that extent misleading to equate, as Davidson does (in *T&M*), a theory of meaning and a theory of truth. For while the inferential consequences of a claim via content rules *are*, in one obvious sense, its truth conditions — *viz*, they are true if it is — it is not truth but rather inferability which is the central notion operative in determinations of synonymy.

I have now isolated three themes traditionally tangled in the language-chess analogy: the notion of a pure normative characterization; the notion of claims as positions and inferences as moves; and the notion of a truth-game, that is, primarily of *entries* to the inferential network of positions developed in the second theme. But, if this development of the language-chess analogy is so far correct, we can now see that the traditional searches for "rules of language" have been looking in the wrong place. And it is precisely this recognition, in fact, which enables us to resolve at last the dilemma we earlier generated from the hypothesis that language is rule-governed.

On the account which I have been elucidating, *entries* are simply linguistic responses to non-linguistic stimuli. In consequence, they are not, in the relevant sense, rule-governed. The critique of rules of language which I investigated earlier took as paradigmatic a rule of the form "Call red things 'red'." and argued that only a person who already spoke a language could obey a rule of that sort. Thus if this was the form of a linguistic rule, one could not *learn* to speak a language. I am now in the position to *grant* that observation, while arguing at the same time that its granting does not imperil the thesis that language-use is a rule-governed — indeed, a rule-constituted — activity.

In order to carry through this argument, however, I shall need a model of language *learning* which is not inductive — that is, which does not presuppose that the learner antecedently possesses sufficient linguistic or quasilinguistic resources to form *hypotheses* about the utterances which he overhears. Now mature language-users, I have suggested, are in command of the rules of language in a full, literal sense. They can speak both a language and a meta-language (and a meta-meta-language, etc. — but that is a complication we can ignore), and, in their metalanguage, they can express norms of semantical correctness for their language. This expression, I suggested, does not typically take the form of explicit rule-normatives — statements of permissions, prohibitions, and injunctions — although it may, but rather is characteristically manifested in the use of the locutions and constructions which I called "terms of semantic appraisal", paradigmatic among these being the subjunctive mood and various applications of the modal auxiliaries. Now the language *learner*, of course, does not *yet* have a command of this normative apparatus. And so he is not subject to its constraints in the way in which a mature speaker is. Yet the constraints are operative in the shaping of his linguistic behavior. How does this come about?

What we know about language learning is scant indeed. Yet a few mountain peaks can be discerned through the fog. The most striking fact is that language learning takes place — apparently quite automatically — when an infant is raised in a mileau of mature language users. What I want to suggest is that this occurs because the linguistic rules of the mature speakers — my "content rules" — have a *double* action-guiding force. Let me illustrate. A sign reads "Bicycle riders must stay on the path". Addressed to me as a bicycle rider, it proposes an explicit "ought-to-do": I ought to ride only on the path. But the sign is, in a certain sense, impersonal, and so I can derive from it, as well, an other-directed "ought-to-*be*": It ought to *be* that other cyclists ride only on the path. And, if the other cyclists and I are, actually or potentially, members of a single community, I may derive from this direct "ought-to-*be*" a second, indirect, "ought-to-*do*" for myself: I ought to do what I can to bring it about that other cyclists ride only on the path.

By speaking of "community" here, I mean to indicate basically a commonality of interest. My behavior and theirs are so interrelated that I derive a (secondary) interest in bringing it about that their behavior conforms to the norms by which I constrain mine in order to further my primary interest — in this case, my interest in cycling.

The subject of an ought-to-do (conduct-normative) must be an agent. But the subject of an ought-to-be (state-normative) need not be. I may, *qua* watch-repairman, hold to the conviction, for example, that Westminster chimes ought to strike on the quarter hour — that is, that it ought to *be* that Westminster chimes strike on the quarter hour. (The example is due to Sellars, *LTC.*) The Westminster chimes of a defective clock cannot, of course, hold the conviction (as a conduct-normative) that they ought to strike on the quarter hour. Westminster chimes cannot obey rules. Yet the obeying of a rule may enter into the explanatory account of the fact that these defective chimes come to strike on the quarter hour, for I may derive from my espoused state-normative the conduct-normative "I ought to bring it about that these defective chimes strike on the quarter hour", and — barring paralysis, akrasia, and similar complications — proceed to do what this self-directed conduct-normative enjoins, *viz.* repair the clock.

We mature speakers and potential language-users in our environment are members of a community in the requisite sense. Our behavior and theirs are so interrelated that we derive a (secondary) interest in bringing it about that their behavior conforms to the norms by which we constrain ours in order to further our (primary) interests — in this case such illocutionary and perlocutionary interests as informing, asking, warning, persuading, and the like. So our espoused linguistic rules generate a secondary state-normative: It ought to be that the linguistic behavior of these non-language-users conforms to the rules which constrain our speaking of our language. And this, in turn, imposes on us a secondary *conduct*-normative: We ought to bring it about that their behavior so conforms.

But what do we do in order to bring this about? Well, the problem is now reduced to one of behavior-shaping, and we know a good deal about that. The infant human is, innately and genetically, a sound-producer; it babbles. One sort of behavior which needs shaping is phonetic behavior. That is surely where things begin. Much of what goes on is pure operant conditioning — the reinforcing of desired behaviors. This happens in myriad subtle ways — gestures, facial expressions, and the like — the most explicit of which is the immediate repetition of the phonemes to be reinforced. Pure operant conditioning continues throughout language learning. From the beginning, it is supplemented by another sort of conditioning which has, to my knowledge, no convenient name (essentially, I suppose, because it can't be applied to rats and pigeons). It is a particular way of responding to incorrect *approximations* to the desired behavior — by immediately producing a *sample or instance* of the correct behavior. Thus a typical conversation between adult and child:

Child: Did you saw the pussycat?

Adult: Did I *see* the pussycat? Yes, I saw it.[5]

Responses of this sort combine negative and positive reinforcement in a complex way. They reinforce verbal behavior in general by being responsive to it. They reinforce features of utterances which are correct by echoing them. Correlatively, they *negatively* reinforce those features of the utterance which are incorrect by providing a *non*-echoic substitute. But this is not arbitrary negative reinforcement, for the substitute provided is the *correct* linguistic form. (This is the part you can't do with rats and pigeons. The experimenter withholds positive reinforcement for behaviors other than the desired operant, but he does not, in those cases, peck the correct key or press the bar himself.) I shall call this 'corrective conditioning'.

The model of language learning which I am providing here is thus, in a sense, evolutionary. What begin as random phoneme strings get structured into larger and larger linguistic units through a process of selective positive reinforcement supplemented by corrective conditioning. (The *details* of this process, as well as the final answer to the question of whether the mechanisms which I have sketched for behavior shaping are by themselves adequate to the task, belong, of course, to psycholinguistics and child psychology, not to philosophy.) Paralleling this development is the reinforcement of *entries* – the shaping of linguistic behavior as a response to *non*-linguistic stimuli. The upshot is that the child's linguistic behavior comes to *conform* to the normatives which our linguistic behavior *obeys*.

It is important to note that this account of language learning presupposes the existence of a speaking community and of the commonalities of interest which give rise to secondary conduct-normatives. It is thus an account which does not generalize to the evolution of language in the *species*, but there is no *a priori* reason to suppose that an adequate account of how *we* learn to speak will do so.

Note, too, that in the initial stages of the process, the language learner is not in command of the relevant rules of language. His behavior is not rule-*obeying* behavior but rather rule-*conforming* behavior. A command of the terms of semantic appraisal will have to be acquired – in application to his *own* linguistic behavior as well as that of others – before the language learner becomes a full-fledged, mature, language-user. This, of course, is not a temporally distinct second stage of language learning, piled upon a completed first stage like a layer on a cake. The acquisition process is the same – and phonetic, syntactic, and semantic aspects of linguistic behavior are all of them shaped simultaneously. The child acquires language and meta-language both, and in the same way – in one mad scramble.

The *explanation* of how it comes about that even the early linguistic behavior of language learners *conforms* to linguistic normatives, however, makes essential reference to the behavior of mature language-users *in obediance to* linguistic normatives. The early behavior of language learners thus lies itself in a sort of middle ground. While not yet rule-obeying behavior, it is equally not *merely* (accidentally) rule-conforming behavior, for its explanation makes essential use of the *notion* of behavior in obediance to rules.

This picture of language learning as behavior shaping combines with my earlier account of rules of language as content rules of inference to accentuate the demand for an account of inference as behavior. It is time to make good that demand. I have earlier claimed that inference is performance. But what kind of a performance is it? In particular, are we not thrown back into the sterility of agent-semantics – inferring joining the closed company of referring, predicating, asserting, meaning, intending, and having in mind? I think not. The key to avoiding this collapse lies in exploiting the notion of a pure normative characterization.

The picture of language learning just sketched views it as multiply-integrative behavior shaping. The behaviors in question are putatively two – entry and inference.[6] In calling the shaping "multiply-integrative", I mean to call attention to the fact, already noted, that these behaviors are conditioned simultaneously, working up random initial productions on the part of the infant into complex behavior conforming to content rules espoused by its linguistic community as conduct-normatives. But there is nothing in this account to require that the behavior thus shaped be *overt* and, indeed, my earlier adoption of an analogical theory of thought allows for *covert*, as well as overt, behavior in conformity to linguistic normatives.[7] Here, however, 'covert' means simply '*in practice* unobservable' and not 'unobservable *in principle*'. For I adopted the stance that, while the language for *describing* thoughts employs (as does a vast amount of the language for describing language) only pure normative characterizations, there must nevertheless *be* structures adequate to and, in fact, answering to these normatively-carved-out functions. In the case of overt language, these structures are sentences – utterance tokens or inscriptions. In the case of thoughts, however, we cannot say in detail what they are – although there is apparently good reason to believe that they will turn out to be electro-chemical conditions of regions of the brain. Fortunately, we have no need to. It is enough to know that language, overt *or* covert, functions representationally in a combinatorial way. For this ensures us that those structures which are thoughts – whatever else they turn out to be – will resemble and differ from one another in ways systematically analogous to the ways in which those overt structures which are *claims* (i.e., sentences) resemble and differ.

We can view, then, language learning as, in extension, the acquisition of a pair of behavioral dispositions — the disposition to respond to non-linguistic stimuli with linguistic behavior (entry) and the disposition to respond to *linguistic* stimuli with linguistic behavior (inference). These are not, in mature language-users, *mere* behavioral dispositions, of course, but they are, in extension, at least that. In both the case of overt speech and the case of thoughts, the linguistic behavior consists in *the production of some item in the natural order*, a natural linguistic object. The only significant difference between the cases will be that, in the case of thoughts, the item produced is a *covert* item. And *that* difference is not relevant to the operation of thought as a system of representations.

Thus the performance which, under a pure normative characterization (intentionally), is *inferring*, say φ from ψ is, in the natural order (extensionally), the production of tokens in a sequence. Specifically, it is responding to a natural linguistic object *normatively* characterizable as a claim (if overt) or a thought (if covert) that ψ by producing a second natural linguistic object *normatively* characterizable as a claim or thought that φ.

And this suggests a convenient fiction. Posit an entity, quite like us in other ways, who has not got the knack of completely covert behavior. All his thinking goes public and, in fact, goes public in the form of *written inscriptions.* Call him "the Author".[8] This is *not* to say that the Author does not engage in that form of covert behavior which is thinking. It is only to say that each covert bit of behavior is precisely mirrored by a bit of overt behavior, the inscribing of a claim.

For the Author, we can, without loss, view entry and inference as behavior in the full, public sense. Entry is claim-inscription upon non-linguistic stimulation, and inference is inscription stimulated by prior inscription. To conform to a content rule is to have a disposition to inscribe, for example, 'x is east of y' having just inscribed 'y is west of x'. For the Author, inference and entry are both public performances, though, to be sure, *causally* backed and mediated by corresponding private (i.e., *in practice covert*) performances.

I argued in Chapter II that to understand how language can represent the world, we must find a sense of 'use' in which 'language-use' cashes out in terms of *real activities*, considered in extension. The inscriptional behavior of the Author is, I submit, language-use in just such a sense. And so I shall take as the raw materials of my analysis of representation these: the regularities of inscriptional behavior exhibited by the Author, and the (*purely extensional*) relationships between the collection of inscriptions (natural linguistic objects) which is the product in the physical world of that activity and that physical world itself, in which the Author moves and lives.

In so doing, I admittedly give priority in *ordo cognoscendi* to something which, in *ordo essendi*, is posterior. But, if I have been so far correct, the priority of thought in the order of being is causal only. Ontologically, thinking and inscribing are one – the producing of physical structures (covert, in one case; overt, in the other) which answer *as well* to certain pure normative characterizations. In the order of *explanation*, we can only understand these structures as representations by first coming to understand their non-representational (extensional) relations to each other and to the wider physical world. Agent-semantics *is* sterile. And this being so, to select as linguistic terms of the analysis the accumulating inscriptions of the Author distorts nothing. For, since his overt tokenings map extensionally one-for-one upon his covert thoughts, the *purely extensional* interrelationships and world-relationships of either collection will be the same. And that, I have argued, is all we need.

CHAPTER IV

TRANSLATION AND THEORIES

I remarked in Chapter I that the fact of a multiplicity of languages raises the question of the extent to which languages are effectively intertranslatable. Since some philosophers, notably Quine, have argued for severe limitations in principle on the enterprise of translation, I concluded that an adequate theory of linguistic representation needed to address itself to the question of the limits of interlinguistic translation. I shall begin this chapter with an investigation of that question and, in particular, of Quine's arguments.

Quine's critique of radical translation in *Word and Object* (and elsewhere) is basically anti-mentalistic in its motivation. His attack is directed at "uncritical semantics",

> ... the myth of a museum in which the exhibits are meanings and the words are labels. To switch languages is to change the labels.

> ... the naturalist's primary objection to this view is not an objection to meanings on account of their being mental entities, though that could be objection enough. The primary objection persists even if we take the labeled exhibits not as mental ideas but as Platonic ideas or even as the denoted concrete objects. Semantics is vitiated by a pernicious mentalism as long as we regard a man's semantics as somehow determinate in his mind beyond what might be implicit in his dispositions to overt behavior. (Quine, *OR*, 186)

Thus parsed, Quine's criticism finds fit object in those theories of the form which I earlier termed "agent-semantics", once their intentionalistic underpinnings have been elicited. In eschewing agent-semantics, it might seem then, I was equally eschewing the uncritical style which Quine wishes to lay to rest. And, with one qualification, this is correct.

The qualification, of course, is this: that, while I do not regard a man's semantics as somehow determinate beyond his dispositions to linguistic behavior, I reject Quine's limitation to *overt* behavior. My position is mentalistic in a sense, for it allows – indeed, it requires – *thoughts*, i.e., in practice covert episodes. But it is not *perniciously* mentalistic, for its model for thinking is inscribing, and it is a keystone of my view that the intentional language of rules and pure normative characterizations must be backed by extensional ontological cash in the form of behavioral dispositions and structures *in re.*

Having made these concessions to the naturalistic point of view, however, there is in consequence, Quine informs us, a price which must be paid. In 'Translation and Meaning' – Chapter II of *Word and Object* – Quine undertakes to

consider how much of language can be made sense of in terms of its stimulus conditions, and what scope this leaves for empirically unconditioned variation in one's conceptual scheme. (*W&O*, 26)

The enterprise with reference to which Quine hopes to highlight the limitations imposed by his naturalistic standpoint is *radical* translation – translation of a hitherto uninvestigated language, unaided by the resemblance of cognate word forms, shared cultural norms, or the services of a bilingual interpreter. His conclusion is that the field linguist who undertakes such an enterprise is, in a sense, doomed to disappointment, not, however, by reason of failing to produce a well-grounded and reasonable translation of the language, but rather by being put in the position of being able to produce an indefinite number of *equally* well-grounded and reasonable translations, all of them mutually incompatible, among which there is nothing to dictate a choice. Specifically,

manuals for translating one language into another can be set up in divergent ways, all compatible with the totality of speech dispositions, yet incompatible with one another. In countless places they will diverge in giving, as their respective translations of a sentence of one language, sentences of the other language which stand to each other in no plausible sort of equivalence however loose. (*W&O*, 27)

This is (one formulation of) the thesis of the indeterminacy of translation.

Translation, argues Quine, is underdetermined by all possible available evidence. What, here, counts as *evidence*? Quine's empirical data-base is precisely what one might expect. What we have to go on is what can be observed of a speaker's linguistic behavior – his public utterances – collated with the conditions under which that behavior takes place – here parsed as the totality of stimuli impinging upon the speaker prior to and simultaneous with the time of his utterance. Application of the techniques of instantial induction equips the field linguist, then, with a set of *speech dispositions* attributable to the speakers of the target language. With this data at his disposal, Quine argues, translation can get off the ground – but only just.

Occasion sentences, sentences which "command assent or dissent only if queried after an appropriate prompting stimulation" (*W&O*, 35–6), can be translated. These are typified by such one-word sentences as 'Rabbit', 'Red', and 'Bachelor'. For those which do not draw heavily on stored collateral information – *observation* sentences (*W&O*, 42) – the linguist can even construct a crude concept of empirical meaning, stimulus meaning, by collecting and classifying stimulations which would prompt a native speaker's assent or dissent (*W&O*, 32). This accomplished, the linguist can proceed to the notion of *stimulus synonymy* or sameness of stimulus meaning of two occasion sentences, a notion which may be broadened and purified in various ways – inter-subjectively when socialized and intra-subjectively when the linguist becomes himself a bilingual, learning the native language as he learned his own when a child. (*W&O*, 46–51) In addition, sentences commanding irreversible assent, *stimulus-analytic* sentences, can be recognized, and truth-functions can be both recognized and translated.

It is, however, when the linguist attempts to move from translation of occasion sentences to translation of terms that, according to Quine, merely practical problems are left behind and serious conceptual difficulties emerge.

[I have so far] stressed that words are learned only by abstraction from their roles in learned sentences. But there are one-word sentences... Insofar as the concept of stimulus meaning may be said to constitute in some strained sense a meaning concept for these, it would seem to constitute a meaning concept for general terms like 'red' and 'rabbit'. This, however, is a mistake. Stimulus synonymy of the occasion sentences 'Gavagai' and 'Rabbit' does not even guarantee that 'gavagai' and 'rabbit' are coextensive terms, terms true of the same things.

For consider 'gavagai'. Who knows but what the objects to which this term applies are not rabbits after all, but mere stages, or brief temporal segments, of rabbits? In either event the stimulus situations that prompt assent to 'Gavagai' would be the same as for 'Rabbit'. Or perhaps the objects to which 'gavagai' applies are all and sundry undetached parts of rabbits; again the stimulus meaning would register no difference. [If]... the linguist leaps to the conclusion that a gavagai is a whole enduring rabbit, he is just taking for granted that the native is enough like us to have a brief general term for rabbits and no brief general term for rabbit stages or parts. (*W&O*, 51–2)

Point to a rabbit and you have pointed to a stage of a rabbit, to an integral part of a rabbit, to the rabbit fusion, and to where rabbithood is manifested... Nothing not distinguished in stimulus meaning itself is to be distinguished by pointing, unless the pointing is accompanied by questions of identity and diversity: 'Is this the same gavagai as that?', 'Do we have here one gavagai or two?'. Such questioning requires of the linguist a command of the native language far beyond anything that we have as yet seen how to account for. (*W&O*, 52–3)

On available intersubjective evidence, then, the linguist can (1) translate observation sentences; (2) translate truth-functions; (3) recognize stimulus-analytic sentences (and their opposites, 'stimulus-contradictory' sentences); and (4) settle questions of intra-subjective stimulus synonymy of occasion sentences if raised (without, however, being able to translate the sentences). But linguists notoriously *do*, in practice, go on to produce sets of term translations for unexplored languages. How, according to Quine, might a linguist proceed to produce such a set of term translations?

In broad outline as follows. He segments heard utterances into conveniently short recurrent parts, and thus compiles a list of native "words." Various of these he hypothetically equates to English words and phrases, in such as way as to conform to (1)–(4). Such are his *analytical hypotheses*, as I call them. (*W&O*, 68)

Taken together, the analytical hypotheses and auxiliary definitions constitute the linguist's jungle-to-English dictionary and grammar. The form they are given is immaterial because their purpose is not translation of words or constructions but translation of coherent discourse; single words and constructions come up for attention only as means to that end. (*W&O*, 70)

It is the linguist's inability to establish, by means other than the employment of analytical hypotheses, the translations of terms (or, correlatively, the translations of non-truth-functional syncategoremata) which, Quine argues, establish his initial thesis of the indeterminacy of translation. He gives us one example of how the indeterminacy might manifest itself in practice.

If by analytical hypothesis we take 'are the same' as translation of some construction in the jungle language, we may proceed on that basis to question our informant about sameness of gavagais from occasion to occasion and so conclude that gavagais are rabbits and not stages. But if instead we take 'are stages of the same animal' as translation of that jungle construction, we will conclude from the same subsequent questioning of our informant that gavagais are rabbit stages. Both analytical hypotheses may be presumed possible. Both could doubtless be accommodated by compensatory variations in analytical hypotheses concerning other locutions, so as to conform equally well to all independently discoverable translations of whole sentences and indeed all speech dispositions of all speakers concerned. And yet countless native sentences admitting of no independent check... may be expected to receive radically unlike and incompatible English renderings under the two systems. (*W&O*, 72)

The thesis of the indeterminacy of translation which thus emerges from Quine's discussions can be put into several different forms. We may say, for example, that Quine holds that there is no avenue of empirical access to the structure of terms, the referential apparatus, and the non-truth-functional syncategoremata — more briefly, to the *categorial structure* — of a second language. Or we may put the thesis differently, in a manner which parallels Quine's original statement of the indeterminacy:

> The infinite totality of sentences in one speaker's language can be mapped onto the total corpus of a second speaker's different language in divergent ways, such that
> (a) the totality of speech dispositions of the first speaker projected by each mapping is invariant, but

(b) the various mappings are not only non-equivalent but actually incompatible with one another.

Now there are several things which should be noted about Quine's argument. What may at first trouble one is that the subjects of the field linguist's studies live in jungles, not cities. What they talk about is rabbits, (or, anyway, Rabbits) and not words. They are, in short, not merely natives but *primitives*, left deliberately unsophisticated. In particular their language *apparently* contains none of the apparatus of semantic appraisal which I earlier moved to the center of my normative stage. Nor, judging from Quine's descriptions of it, does it contain explicit metalinguistic machinery. It may seem, then, that what indeterminacy there is in the translation procedure is adventitious and that the missing evidence is missing only in practice, not in principle. Thus supplement the native community with, for example, a cluster of *philosophers* who continue and enrich the linguistic education of our field investigator by instructing him further in the native tongue until he is able to read fluently and converse intelligently about *native* philosophical works and disputes paralleling those in which Quine *et al* dissect the apparatus of divided reference characteristic of English and distinguish it from other possible categorial structures. The linguist would then have acquired a further set of speech dispositions — dispositions to semantic discourse and the drawing of categorial distinctions — and it may seem that this enrichment of his data-base can leave no residual indeterminacy of choice among his analytical hypotheses. To argue in this way, however, is to mistake the character of Quine's critique.

Quine's language at times suggests that the indeterminacy in question is an *operational* indeterminacy. Available evidence is insufficient to *determine* which of pair of competing analytical hypotheses is correct — although one or another among the various possible hypotheses *is* correct. Thinking of the thesis of translational indeterminacy in this way leads to the suggestion that all that is needed is *more* evidence of the same *general* kind. But this is not Quine's view. He holds that evidence of *that* kind — intersubjectively available evidence concerning speech dispositions and their stimulus conditions — however extensive, cannot *in principle* decide among competing analytical hypotheses. And this is not a mere operational limitation. Rather, it obtains because there *is* no correct decision to be arrived at.

The point is not that we cannot be sure whether the analytical hypothesis is right, but that there is not even, as there was in the case of [the occasion sentence] 'Gavagai', an objective matter to be right or wrong about. (*W&O*, 73)

It is not that the linguist is unable to arrive at the truth of the matter. There *is* no truth of the matter.

Yet what is the pattern of argument here? Why should we not suppose that it is only radical *operational* inaccessibility which has been located by Quine's considerations? Part of the answer can surely be gotten by recurring to Quine's views on "uncritical semantics". For to suppose a truth of the matter here is to suppose the mythical museum, one might argue – only now with cases of opaque glass. Yet, in the end, what stands in the way of this supposition?

Surely it must be some such commitment as this: That a putative supposition *makes no sense* (is empty, is vacuous) if there is no way of coming to know, even in principle, whether it is correct or incorrect. In more traditional terminology: a putative claim which is in principle unverifiable and unfalsifiable is meaningless. To argue, in other words, as Quine does, from the demonstrable failure of an epistemological inquiry to the non-existence of the putative object of that inquiry (thus, to the non-existence of a single correct translation of the native tongue) is to espouse some version of a verification principle, not, of course, in the traditional sense – for Quine eschews meanings and, thus, eschews the identification of the meaning of a claim with its method of verification – but in the sense in which verification principles have been argued to underlie the Private Language Argument and transcendental deductions.[1] It is some such principle as this which, in the end, is operative in Quine's rejection of "uncritical semantics" and the myth of mentalism *on the basis* of his epistemological critique of the enterprise of radical translation. But let me defer further discussion of this point and recur to the main line of argument.

In 1967 (*SEL*), I argued that Quine's thesis of the indeterminacy of translation is incompatible with his simultaneously espoused thesis of the *determinacy* of *intra*-linguistic semantic studies, viz:

The indeterminacy of translation invests even the question of what objects to construe a term as true of. Studies of the semantics of reference consequently turn out to make sense only when directed upon substantially our language, from within. But we do remain free to reflect, thus parochially, on the development and structure of our own referential apparatus... (*W&O*, ix)

Specifically, I argued that we are no worse off with respect to two languages than we are with respect to two *idiolects* of what is *phonetically* one language. The hypothesis of the indeterminacy of translation, in other words, entails that

The infinite totality of sentences in one speaker's idiolect can be mapped onto the total corpus of a second speaker's homophonic idiolect in divergent ways such that,

(a) the totality of speech dispositions of the first speaker projected by each mapping is invariant, but

(b) the various mappings are not only non-equivalent but actually incompatible with one another.

I took this to be a *reductio* of Quine's position in the classical vein, for the truth of *this* thesis would undercut his ability to *argue* for it. How, after all, could I know whether what Quine's term 'rabbit' refers to is what is referred to by *my* (like-sounding) term 'rabbit' or rather by my 'rabbit stage', 'rabbit fusion', or what have you? How, in fact, could I decide whether what Quine refers to as "the same language" is not what I refer to as "stages of the same language"?

In fact, as I later came to realize, the problem is even more radical, for what is true *synchronically* of two speakers' homophonic idiolects is true *diachronically* of a single speaker's homophonic idiolects at different times in his history. One arrives, in other words, at "referential solipsism of the present moment". But, if this is so, there is no such thing as *the* referential apparatus of the English language. Thus the thesis of determinacy of intralinguistic semantics must be false. And, if *that* be rejected, Quine can no longer specify *what it is* that the radical translator fails to accomplish, what it is that he cannot do. Thus the truth of the thesis of indeterminacy of translation undermines the ability to espouse it.

In what Carnap would call the material mode, the indeterminacy of translation, which began as a critique of meaning, becomes the inscrutability of reference.

The terms 'rabbit', 'undetached rabbit part', and 'rabbit stage' differ not only in meaning; they are true of different things. Reference itself proves behaviorally inscrutable. (*OR*, 191)

In 1968, Quine could be found arguing what I argued in 1967. But he did not take it to be a *reductio* of his position. He took it to be his position.

On deeper reflection, radical translation begins at home. Must we equate our neighbor's English words with the same strings of phonemes in our own mouths? Certainly not... The homophonic rule is a handy one on the whole ... [but] we can systematically reconstrue our neighbor's apparent reference to rabbits as really references to rabbit stages... We can reconcile all this with our neighbor's verbal behavior, by cunningly readjusting our translations of his various connecting predicates so as to compensate for the switch of ontology. In short, we can reproduce the inscrutability of reference at home.

I have urged... that the inscrutability of reference is not the inscrutability of a fact; there is no fact of the matter. But if there is really no fact of the matter, then the inscrutability of reference can be brought even closer to home than the neighbor's case; we can apply it to ourselves...

We seem to be maneuvering ourselves into the absurd position that there is no difference on any terms, interlinguistic or intralinguistic, between referring to rabbits and referring to rabbit parts or stages... Surely this is absurd, for it would imply that there is no difference between the rabbit and each of its parts or stages... Reference would seem now to become nonsense not just in radical translation, but at home. (*OR*, 199–200)

Quine's solution to this quandary is to eschew questions of absolute reference entirely. Rather, we are to take some background language as a "coordinate system" and regress into it, much as, in physics, we locate positions and velocities only relative to some given coordinate system.

It is meaningless to ask whether, in general, our terms 'rabbit', 'rabbit part', 'number', etc. really refer respectively to rabbits, rabbit parts, numbers, etc., rather than to some ingeniously permuted denotations. It is meaningless to ask this absolutely; we can meaningfully ask it only relative to some background language. (*OR*, 200)

But regresses have a way of perniciously iterating themselves. Does Quine's become one of these problematic, vicious infinite regresses?

When we are given position and velocity relative to a given coordinate system, we can always ask in turn about the placing of the origin and axes of that system of coordinates; and there is no end to the succession of further coordinate systems that could be adduced in answering the successive questions thus generated.

In practice of course we end the regress of coordinate systems by something like pointing. And in practice we end the regress of background language, in discussions of reference, by acquiescing in our mother tongue and taking its words at face value. (*OR*, 201)

Yet, when we point, we point to some *actual location*, something which *can* do fit service as the origin of a coordinate system. Inscrutability of reference, however, is, on Quine's view, not inscrutability of a fact. And if there is no fact of the matter, then there is nothing *to* take at face value. Nothing is elucidated by mapping the inscrutable onto the inscrutable. As Ramsey nicely put it (*FM*, 238): "What we can't say we can't say, and we can't whistle it either." Quine here fails fully to appreciate the consequences of his own inscrutability thesis. To terminate the regress of background languages in our own "taken at face value" is to cash a forged check with counterfeit currency. If "reference *is* nonsense except relative to a coordinate system" (*OR*, 200), it does no good to *pretend* that, of course, reference in the coordinate system isn't *really* nonsense.

The thesis of the indeterminacy of translation and its corollary, the inscrutability of reference, I conclude, are irremediably self-refuting. And so there must be something wrong with the reasoning which leads to them. Yet surely Quine's epistemological naturalism is well-taken.

Language is a social art. In acquiring it we have to depend entirely on intersubjectively available cues as to what to say and when. Hence there is no justification for collating linguistic meanings, unless in terms of men's dispositions to respond overtly to socially observable stimulations. (*W&O*, ix)

Quine is surely right about the field linguist's data-base. If he is wrong about the limits of radical translation, then, he must be mistaken about the modes of empirical inference licensing conclusions grounded in this data-base. And I think that this is so. Quine insists that the indeterminacy in question is *peculiarly* linguistic. His models, however, sometimes suggest the contrary. One key diagnostic passage is this:

The notable point about the analytical hypotheses was that two independent Martians could acquire perfect and indistinguishable English through unlike and even incompatible systems of English-to-Martian analytical hypotheses. The corresponding point about English children is that two of them may attain to an identical command of English through very dissimilar processes of tentative association and adjustment of the various interdependent adjectives and particles on which the trick of divided reference depends. (*W&O*, 94)

Yet, as Quine would like to interpret his thesis of translational indeterminacy, the two points are not at all "corresponding", for the English children *do*, and the Martian linguists *do not* get on to "the trick of divided reference". If we take Quine literally, in other words, we find that the term 'English' is here being used ambiguously. The "English" which the English children acquire is a language with a *determinate referential apparatus*, but the "English" which the Martians acquire is not a language with determinate categorial structure, but simply a system of overt speech dispositions and phonological manipulations. Whereas the case of the English children fits the pattern

(I)   There is such a thing as the English language over and above what can be determined by phonological analysis. It has a determinate referential apparatus which is learnable and, in fact, learned.

What is undetermined by available intersubjective evidence is that pattern of conditionings and that set of neural hookups by means of which the individual speaker has acquired his *de facto* command of this, referentially determinate, English language;

the case of the Martian linguists requires

(II)   There is nothing which can properly be described as *the* English
             language acquired by the Martians over and above what can be
             determined by phonological analysis. Identical phonological
             systems yielding identical patterns of speech dispositions *have*
             no underlying determinate referential structure to be learned.

             Available intersubjective evidence gives one no grounds for
             singling out any one referential apparatus as *the* referential
             apparatus of English.

Perhaps, then, if Quine can confuse the trivial indeterminacy in (I) with
the striking – but, I have argued, non-existent – indeterminacy of (II), he is
wrong as well about the unique character of translational indeterminacy.
For there is a *general* indeterminacy characteristic of *empirical* theories as
such. Any physical (matter-of-factual, empirical) theory is underdetermined
by the totality of evidence intersubjectively available at any given time.[2]
This is most strikingly evident in the practice of drawing smooth curves
through small finite sets of data points, but manifestations of it are common
enough elsewhere, and it has not, I think, been seriously contested. Perhaps,
then, what Quine has uncovered in his investigations of the epistemology of
linguistics is simply another – particularly impressive – instance of this
general empirical indeterminacy.

   Indeed, there are striking analogies between Quine's stance in the philosophy of language and certain venerable positions in the philosophy of
physics. Recall that the term translations projected by a set of analytical
hypotheses, on Quine's account, come in only as a calculating device. Any
set of analytical hypotheses which projects native utterances into linguists'
utterances with matching stimulus conditions will do, and no such set is to
be preferred to any other. One is reminded here of the instrumentalistic
viewpoint with respect to unobservable entities in physics. Talk about, say,
electrons, the instrumentalist holds, comes in only as a convenient
calculating device for predicting observable experimental outcomes given
observable experimental setups. There is, he would hold, no right or wrong
about electrons – no fact of the matter – but only the question of the
utility of electron-theory (electron *talk*) for predicting observable correlations of observables.

   Now this standpoint makes sense, I wish to argue, only against the background of certain views about the aims and character of empirical inquiry.
In particular, what underlies instrumentalism in the physical sciences is the

picture of physical inquiry conducted according to the *hypothetico-deductive method*. On this view, the ultimate aims of physical inquiry are the prediction and control of natural phenomena; the proximate aim, the discovery of true empirical generalizations correlating observables with observables in a way which allows prediction and, ideally, gives a handle on the problem of control. The method advocated for attaining these aims is, provisionally, this: One begins by collecting *data*. Sufficient data suggest an *hypothesis*.[3] Thus the "hypothetico-" part of the rubric. The next step is to *test* the hypothesis. To test an hypothesis, one first *deduces a prediction*. Thus the "deductive" part of the rubric. One then observes to determine whether or not the prediction is borne out. What happens next depends upon the result of this observation. If the prediction is not borne out, one concludes that the hypothesis is *falsified*. It is then to be categorically excluded from one's stock of empirical beliefs, and one re-enters the methodological algorithm at either the data-gathering or hypothesis-forming step. If, on the other hand, the prediction *is* borne out, one concludes that the hypothesis has received some *confirmation* (not, however, that it is verified). It may then be *provisionally* added to one's stock of empirical beliefs and the methodological algorithm re-entered at the testing step by the deduction of another prediction. Falsification is absolute; confirmation admits of degrees. Rejection of an hypothesis is absolute; acceptance is always provisional.

Thus the aim of the enterprise, prediction, is viewed as the driving force of its method. An explanation, on this way of looking at things, is ancillary. It is, in essence, a prediction after the fact. Like the testing of hypotheses, explanation proceeds by deduction. A particular phenomenon is said to be explained when a statement of its occurrence can be deduced from highly confirmed empirical hypotheses (now called "laws") in conjunction with true statements of initial conditions. And an empirical generalization (law) is said to be explained when it can itself be deduced from a law or set of laws of higher generality. The notion of a *theory*, on this account, is essentially epiphenomenal. A theory is simply a *set* of generalizations (hypotheses or laws) sharing a distinctive vocabulary.

This methodological standpoint does not, of course, by itself give rise to the instrumentalism canvassed briefly above – the view that unobservable entities are logical fictions. But instrumentalism is an immediate consequence of its combination with something like the verification principle elicited earlier from Quine's arguments for the indeterminacy thesis. The hypothetico-deductive method allows for falsification, but not verification, of hypotheses. If one holds, then, that the semantic content of an empirical

hypothesis is exhausted by the set of its possible observational verifications
(the strong form of the verification principle), one will deny talk putatively
about unobservable entities full referential status. Its utility, then, must be
instrumental rather than representational.

Quine, in general, shares these methodological commitments.

We may think of the physicist as interesting in systematizing such general truths as can
be said in common-sense terms about ordinary physical things. . . . A sufficient reason
for his positing extraordinary physical things, viz. molecules and subvisible groups of
molecules, is that for the thus-supplemented universe he can devise a theory θ' which is
simpler than θ and agrees with θ in its consequences for ordinary things. Its further
consequences for his posited extraordinary things are incidental. (*W&O*, 21)

Having thus embraced instrumentalism in physical theory, it is not surprising to find Quine hewing to it in linguistic theory as well. Yet the arguments
and methodological conceptions which form the underpinnings of this
standpoint are deeply suspect. I have already marked the critical role of
verification principles, both in Quine's conclusions and in the development
of the instrumentalist position. The reservations about principles of this sort
are familiar and widely known, too familiar and too widely known to bear
another careful canvassing here. What is, perhaps, not so familiar and widely
known – although becoming daily moreso – is a set of considerations con-
ducing to the conclusion that the received account of scientific methodology is through-and-through mistaken. The initial impetus for these considerations is extrinsic to philosophical theorizing, deriving from careful
studies of the history of science. A detailed examination of a familiar, but
relevant, example will help to make the necessary points.

Newton's three Laws of Motion, in conjunction with his Law of Universal
Gravitation, constitute a long-standing exemplar of physical science at its
best and purest. Traditionally, they are supposed to have several virtues.
Collectively, they have been held to *explain*, for example, Kepler's Laws of
Planetary Motion and Galileo's Law of Falling Bodies. Yet a bit of careful
consideration reveals straightaway that they do not, indeed, *cannot* do so if
explanation be construed on the classical (Hempelian) model as deduction.
(See, e.g., Hempel and Oppenheim, *LE.*) Newton's Law of Universal Gravitation states that any body in the universe attracts any other body with a
force directly proportional to the product of their masses and inversely
proportional to the square of the distance between them. ($F = Gm_1 m_2/d^2$)
The orbital motion of a planet and the falling of a body near the surface of
the earth are accelerated motions. The connexion with universal gravitation
is made through Newton's Second Law: Acceleration is directly proportional to the applied force and inversely proportional to the mass of the

accelerating body. ($F = ma$) Galileo's Law of Falling Bodies states that the acceleration of a body in free-fall near the surface of the earth is constant ($a = g$) and, consequently the distance traversed by such a body is directly proportional to the square of the elapsed time ($s = \frac{1}{2}gt^2$). Traditionally, Newton is supposed to have explained this law by identifying the acceleration of a body in free-fall as an acceleration resulting solely from the gravitational force exerted on the body by the earth. The explanatory deduction, then, supposely proceeds as follows:

> The force resulting from the gravitational attraction of the earth is $F = Gm_0 m_e/r^2$, where m_0 is the mass of the object, m_e the mass of the earth, and r the radius of the earth. The force producing an acceleration equal to a is, by the Second Law, $F = m_0 a$. Setting these forces equal, we have $m_0 a = Gm_0 m_e/r^2$ whereupon, dividing both sides of this equation by m_0 we obtain $a = Gm_e/r^2$ which is constant, given that both the mass of the earth and its radius are fixed.

What is wrong here, of course, is that the distance separating the centers of gravity of the falling object and the earth is not equal to the radius of the earth, r. In fact, the distance is a constantly changing one equal to r plus some function of time, f(t) which, in fact, Galileo's Law itself allows us to *approximate* $- d \approx r + s_0 - \frac{1}{2}gt^2$, where s_0 is the initial distance of the object from the surface of the earth. Putting this observation back into the argument yields $a = Gm_e/(r + f(t))^2$ which, rather than positing a *constant* acceleration in accord with Galileo's Law of Falling Bodies, posits an acceleration which varies continuously in a time-dependent fashion during free-fall. Rather than entailing the truth of Galileo's Law, in other words, Newton's Laws entail its literal falsity. For Galileo's Law is *inconsistent* with Newton's theory.

A similar result obtains regarding Kepler's Laws of Planetary Motion. His first law, for example, states that the orbit of a planet about the sun is an ellipse with the sun at one focus. Something quite like this can, in fact, be deduced from Newton's Laws. Specifically, it can be shown that the motion of a body resulting solely from the action of a single central gravitational force is accelerated motion answering to Kepler's descriptions. The difficulty here, of course, is that the motion of a planet about the sun is not such motion. For Newton's Law of Universal Gravitation is literally universal in scope, and thus any planet is subject, not merely to the central solar gravitational force, but to an indeterminate, though very large, set of forces resulting from the gravitational attractions of other planets, meteors, asteroids, remote stars, interstellar clouds of gas and dust, and occasional random hydrogen atoms. True, the central gravitational force is the *major* determinant of planetary motion, but between "major determinant" and "sole determinant" is a great gap fixed – and it is precisely this gap which lies between the supposed *deducibility* of Kepler's Laws from Newton's, given actual initial conditions, and the actual *inconsistency* of Kepler's Laws with Newton's, given those same initial conditions. Perturbational forces on a planet being what Newton's theory says they must be, it *cannot* be the case that the orbital motion of that planet about the sun *is* (rather than "approximates to") an ellipse.

Given, then, that the traditional account fails on the side of explanation, we should not be so surprised to find that it fails, as well, on the side of confirmation and falsification. Just this, indeed, is what attention to the history of science reveals. A prediction of the position of the planet Uranus was calculated according to Newton's Laws, due allowance being made for known perturbational forces. Although Newton's Theory was, by this time, highly confirmed, scrupulous astronomical observations failed to bear out the calculated prediction. The observed position of Uranus differed from its computed position by a factor too large to be assimilated to experimental or observational error. On the traditional account, the method enjoins rejection of the espoused hypothesis from which the failed prediction has been deduced. Newton's Theory had been shown to entail an incorrect prediction, so Newton's Theory must go. But the course in fact chosen independently by Adams and by Leverrier was a different one.

Holding Newton's Theory as a fixed point, they concluded that – as the principles of the theory dictated – Uranus' observed deviation from its predicted position must be due to a hitherto unsuspected perturbational gravitational force. They proceeded then to *use* the theory to calculate the probable position of a planet the presence of which would suitably explain the observed anomaly in the orbit of Uranus. And, in the case of Uranus, the gambit worked; Neptune showed up as predicted.

In the case of the 40″ of arc deviation from the predicted value for the perihelion of Mercury, however, the analogous gambit – attempting to locate a hypothetical planetary body, Vulcan, the perturbational gravitational effects of which would account for the observed deviation – failed to work. Vulcan did not show up as predicted. Yet even this strong failure of predictivity did not lead to the rejection of Newtonian dynamics. Practicing physicists clung tenaciously to the theory. The 40″ of arc deviation was entered on the books as an *unexplained anomaly* in the orbit of Mercury.

And there the phenomenon rested, until Einstein's successor to Newton's theory explained it.

These are, by now, commonplaces of the history of science. But what they suggest is that the traditional picture of scientific methodology is radically mistaken. An entrenched theory apparently cannot be dislodged by recalcitrant observations. Its test is not, apparently, its ability to exceptionlessly yield predictions borne out by subsequent observation. Nor apparently does explanation fit the Hempelian deductive model. What is needed is a totally new picture of the scientific method — one which fits the facts. And such a picture is emerging.[4]

The argument against the notion of a crucial experiment — a failed prediction which conclusively falsifies an hypothesis or theory — was, in essence, given by Duhem (*ASPT*). A theory, T, entails a prediction, P, only in conjunction with certain posits regarding standing and initial conditions, C. Thus: C&T → P. The failure of the prediction P to be borne out, then, allows us to infer only the falsehood of the conjunction C&T. And this, in turn, permits us to conclude that C is false *or* T is false. But it does not permit any further isolation of the error. Thus we remain always *free* to conclude that its locus lies in C rather than in T. This, we have seen, was the course chosen by Adams and Leverrier. They rejected, not Newton's Theory, but the background assumption that all perturbational forces acting upon Uranus sufficient to produce a positional deviation of a certain magnitude were known.

A clause of this sort is *always* tacit in the application of any theory. For any theory encompasses only a fixed and finite number of parameters within its scope. In applying the theory, then, one is tacitly presupposing that the parameters dealt with by the theory are the only parameters *relevant* to determination of the phenomenon being predicted. Where this is, to the appropriate degree of approximation, correct, something like the gambit employed by Adams and Leverrier will work. Where it is not correct, however, extant theory cannot be used to explain the deviation of an observation from its predicted value. Here what is required is a new theory, one which takes into account parameters — thus, for example, relativistic effects — not treated by its predecessor.

This observation generalizes in another way. Any theory fits any set of data with a certain amount of slack. In particular, laws come with a presumption of *limit conditions* — limiting values for certain theoretical parameters outside of which there is no expectation that the relationships posited by the laws continue to hold. One way in which a new theory can improve upon its predecessor, then, is by extending range of application beyond the prior limit conditions. And in order to do this, it must isolate

certain features of the empirical situation in virtue of which application of
the predecessor laws failed outside of those limits.

The picture which begins to emerge from these considerations is this: We
have, first, a *theoretical wholism* already arising on Duhemian grounds. Just
as hypotheses cannot be tested in isolation from posits concerning standing
and initial conditions, they equally cannot be tested in isolation from background posits constituted by other theoretical relationships among the parameters being investigated tacitly held fixed. Thus, for example, failures of
predictions based upon Newton's Theory reflect equally upon the Laws of
Motion and the Law of Universal Gravitation, and, if anything, it is the
theoretical system composed of all the Newtonian laws relating mass, force,
velocity, and acceleration which is called into question by recalcitrant observations.

Second, what it takes to dislodge an accepted theory turns out to be a
better theory. Leaving in abeyance for a moment the question of what sense
of 'better' is here at issue, it is sufficient to note that the availability of
Duhemian qualms, particularly with respect to the tacit posit that the parameters treated of by extant theory are the sole parameters relevant to determination of the predicted phenomenon, stands in the way of straightforward observational falsification of a theory. What is needed is a total
theoretical structure which can do the job better than the extant theory
which it supplants.

But what is this job? Well, this much at least is clear: It is not *simply* the
job of facilitating accurate predictions of observable phenomena. A Ptole-
maic theory of epicycles, for example, admits of continuous refinement to
produce predictions of planetary positions accurate to any desired degree of
precision. If accuracy of prediction were the end of the matter, such continuous epicyclic refinements would seem to be enjoined by the canons of
the method. Again, just as Galileo's Law of Falling Bodies is not shown false
by a failed prediction in a college physics laboratory, so equally repeated
predictive successes in such a context lend it no further credibility than
Galileo's initial experiments. It is a striking fact about theory confirmation,
in fact, that, when experiment is called for, one or two observations will
generally do the job. A physical theory seems to acquire and lose credibility
in quantum jumps, not piecemeal and gradually as classical confirmation
theory would have it. How is this to be understood?

All of these epistemological phenomena become intelligible if we move
explanation, rather than prediction, to the center of the stage. Physical
theorizing does not occur in ignorance. When we come to test a theory having in its scope a range of phenomena, then, I suggest that the test of the

theory will be the extent to which it *explains what we already know* about the phenomena. If this is so, it will itself explain what we have observed about scientific methodology. If explanatory, rather than predictive, utility is the prime desideratum of a physical theory, we would not *expect* failed predictions to refute an established theory. For the theory was accepted on the grounds that it explained a certain range of phenomena. Its failure to predict certain *other* phenomena, then, does not *per se* undermine its credibility as an explanation of the *original* phenomena. What is required to supercede an explanation of a certain range of phenomena is a *better explanation* of those phenomena. And so we should expect one theory to be superceded only by another at least as great in explanatory scope.

In the pure case, what we already know about a range of phenomena is already codified as a theory of those phenomena. If explanation were deduction, we should expect our successor theory to entail the truth of its predecessor(s). Yet we have already noted that, standardly, far from implying it, the truth of the new theory is *inconsistent* with the truth of the old. How then can a successor theory explain "what we already know" about a range of phenomena when "what we already know" is encapsulated in our predecessor theory?

Well, what in detail *is* the relationship between, say, Newton's Theory and those of Kepler and Galileo? The literal truth of Newton's Theory entails the literal falsehood of Kepler's and Galileo's, to be sure. But the literal truth of Newton's Theory entails also the *approximate truth* of Kepler's and Galileo's. If, contrary to fact, a planet were acted upon solely by the central solar gravitational force, its motion would be as Kepler's Laws describe it. And if, contrary to fact, the distance between the centers of gravity of the earth and a falling body remained constant, the acceleration of that body resulting from the gravitational attraction of the earth would be constant. Now a planet is *not* acted upon solely by the central solar gravitational force, but that force *is* significantly larger than the sum of the various perturbational forces, a sum which the theory also allows one to calculate. For the masses of *local* perturbational bodies (planets, asteroids, and the like) are orders of magnitude smaller than the mass of the sun, and perturbational bodies of stellar magnitude (viz. the "fixed stars") lie at distances many orders of magnitude greater than the distance from any planet to the sun. Since perturbational force varies directly with mass and inversely with the square of distance, Newton's theory yields the result that the perturbational forces which it posits are very small in comparison to central solar gravitation. In consequence, the deviation of a planetary orbit from the conditions laid down in Kepler's Laws will be near vanishingly small.

Similarly, while the distance between the centers of gravity of a falling body and the earth are constantly changing in a time-dependent fashion, the ratio of the radius of the earth to the distance of a body in free-fall near the surface of the earth from the earth's center remains very close to 1. The deviation of the actual acceleration from the constant value predicted by Galileo's Law will thus again be near vanishingly small.

What a successor theory explains, then, is the *descriptive success* of its predecessor(s). It explains why objects obey the predecessor laws *to the extent that they have been observed to do so*. It does this by offering a new set of laws (and, in interesting cases, even a new set of objects interestingly related to the old) which objects are held *literally* – though, since the new theory is always open for future revision, provisionally – to obey. In terms of the principles of the new theory, one can show that the empirical situation now posited as actually obtaining is a good approximation to the empirical situation posited by the predecessor theory. Frequently this is accomplished by showing the predecessor situation to be an idealization of the newly posited actual situation. (Kepler is right, if perturbational forces equal 0; Galileo is right, discounting small changes in relative distance.) Correlative to the explanation of predecessor theory success is the explanation of predecessor theory failure. The new theory must not only explain why objects obey the predecessor laws to the extent which they have been found to do so, it must also make some advance on explaining why they *fail* to obey predecessor laws to the extent that they have been found *not* to do so. That is, the successor theory must make some advance on explaining the limit conditions of the predecessor laws. And this is accomplished by isolating the empirical features of the limit situations in virtue of which they deviate from the situations in which the predecessor laws serve as good approximations and giving a theoretical account of the contributions of these features to the behavior of the objects of the theory.

Once we understand the central role of explanation in theory succession and confirmation, and once we have separated explanation from its Hempelian deductive model,[5] we can see, too, the proper role of prediction in theory confirmation. What needs to be understood is why one or two predictions will do the confirmatory job, and why it is the case that repeated predictive successes of a certain sort do not increase the credibility of an hypothesis beyond that yielded by certain initial experiments. The solution of these puzzles is to tie the notion of prediction to that of explanation. When one is adjudicating between predecessor and successor theories, one is possessed of two explanatory accounts of a range of empirical phenomena between which one seeks a decision. Predictions may be helpful here, but not just any predictions will do. Predictions, for example, that gases will obey the Boyle-Charles Law with a certain degree of accuracy add no support to the kinetic (molecular) theory of gases, even though the kinetic theory entails that gases will obey the Boyle-Charles Law with that degree of accuracy. The predictions selected for theory confirmation must *adjudicate* between rival theoretical *descriptions*. They can do this only if what is predicted are phenomena which the successor theory can, and the predecessor theory cannot, *explain*. What a *relevantly* successful prediction shows us is that the actual empirical situation is what the successor theory describes it as being rather than what is posited by the predecessor theory. And it cannot do this unless the predicted phenomenon falls within the *explanatory* range of the successor theory but outside the explanatory range of the predecessor. Having found a prediction of this sort, however, it is enough — barring procedural error — that it be borne out just once. For what is at issue is the actual character of the empirical situation. Once it is established that the behavior of objects in certain empirical conditions is, *in fact*, such as can be explained by the successor theory and not by the predecessor, further predictions of that sort become redundant. Greater predictive scope, thus, functions as an indication of greater explanatory scope. It is not, as the classical account would have it, that explanation is ancillary to predictive power. Rather, it is that the predictive reach of a theoretical account establishes the actual empirical situation to answer to the successor descriptions rather than to those of the predecessor by mapping the comparative boundaries of the *explanatory* reach of the two theories.

I am now some distance away from the initial questions of translation with which I began this chapter, but it is easy enough to return to them. Quine is through-and-through committed to the classical picture of scientific methodology. His hypothesized field linguist wishes to *predict* (dispositions to) observable speech behavior given observable stimulus conditions. I should like, however, to regard the translator's analytical hypotheses as forming, collectively, a *theory* of the native language. The model here will not be *macro*-theories of the astronomical sort but rather postulational *micro*-theories of the sort typified by the molecular theory of gases or the genetic theory of inherited traits. Theories of this sort have a double subject matter. From their predecessors, they inherit their *external* subject matter — thus for example, gases in the case of the kinetic theory. The postulations which constitute their explanatory bases stipulate their *internal* subject matter — thus for example, molecules in the kinetic theory. Finally, observable features of the external subject matter are identified as specific functions of the postulated characteristics of the (unobservable) internal subject matter – thus for example, temperature as the mean kinetic energy of a molecule in a sample of gas. From this point, the situation is as it was for macro-theories. The successor micro-theory explains the descriptive successes of its predecessor macro-theory by deriving, within the successor theory, counterparts of the predecessor laws, typically under idealizing initial conditions (thus for example, that molecules have diameter 0 and that collisions between molecules are perfectly elastic). And it explains descriptive failures of the predecessor macro-theory by isolating features of the (newly posited) actual empirical situation which contribute to the deviations of observed phenomena from predecessor generalizations and by calculating the effects of this contribution.

In the case of translation, the totality of determinable dispositions to observable speech behavior constitutes the analogue of the external subject matter of a postulational theory. And corresponding to the postulated micro-entities and micro-properties of a physical theory – its internal subject matter – will be the categorial structure, the set of term translations and the referential apparatus, which is projected for the native language by a set of analytical hypotheses. The thesis of translational indeterminacy, then, has a counterpart thesis of *theoretical* indeterminacy: For any given body of physical phenomena, there exists a pair of *equally good* yet incompatible physical theories.

The "goodness" in question here is the goodness of *theories*. And everything turns upon what one makes of it. If the goodness of a theory is taken to be constituted by its *predictive utility*, Quine may well be right. ("*May be right*" since, as we shall see, he actually offers no *argument* to support this claim.) In the case of physical theories, however, Quine's thesis is more guarded:

... we have no reason to suppose that man's surface irritations even unto eternity admit of any one systematization that is scientifically better or simpler than all possible others. (*W&O*, 23)

Continuous epicyclic refinement of *any* account is, after all, always possible on an *ad hoc* basis. If all that is wanted is a maximally accurate instrument of prediction, then, continuous refinement of any theoretical account will, in principle, do as well as continuous refinement of any other. The most that could be said in favor of one such refinement is that it is *simpler in application* than another, and Quine correctly sees that it is difficult to argue on *a priori* grounds for a connection between simplicity and truth.

But I have been arguing that it is a mistake to take the goodness of a theory as predictive utility. Rather it is the *explanatory* power of a theory which is crucial. Prediction enters the methodology of science as the hand-maiden of explanation, the testing of inferred predictions being essentially an instrument for isolating the character of the actual empirical situation by mapping the relative *explanatory* ranges of a pair of competing theories which purport to describe it. If this is so, then, there *can* be something to choose among competing theories and, in the long run, there *must* be. For once we recognize that a theory does its explanatory job by giving an account of what the *actual* empirical situation *is*, the fact that a pair of in-compatible competing theories of apparently equal explanatory power apply over a range of physical phenomena becomes the best reason we could have for believing that we have not yet finished the theoretical task. For that phenomena are such as to allow of being described by incompatible theories with apparently equal claims to correctness *is itself a fact which stands in need of explanation.* We need, in other words, a successor theory which explains *why it is* that these incompatible competitor-theories are equally successful, where they are so. And this explanation will take the same form as the explanation of the descriptive success of a single predeces-sor theory — giving a redescription of the actual empirical situation which allows an account of the successes and failures now of *two* predecessors by providing counterpart models of *both* within the successor theory and facilitating the inference of counterpart laws for the predecessor laws of *each* of the incompatible predecessors within the successor theory under (possibly very different) idealizing assumptions concerning initial con-ditions.

A correct understanding of scientific methodology, then, gives us not only a way of choosing among incompatible theories of equal predictive reach, but a good argument *a priori* for the conclusion that, in the long run, there must be a *single* systematizing theory. Theories cannot continue to proliferate and diverge with equal claim to acceptability precisely because the fact of a single such divergence is itself a phenomenon the accounting for which is a constraint on any acceptable immediate successor theory.

Applying these considerations to Quine's translation problem, we find that only the residual and trivial indeterminacy of any empirical inquiry remains. (This is the indeterminacy imported by the fact that any theory is underdetermined by any finite data set available at a given time.) Methodo-logically, then, I stand more with Chomsky than with Quine. The Chomskian linguist aims at explaining how native speakers of a language are *able* to do what they have been *observed* to do — to disambiguate utter-ances, recognize what is being said, mark certain utterances as anomalous, and assess certain grammatical descriptions as better than others. This is the point of Chomsky's talk about *competences* and his criteria of descriptive and explanatory adequacy (*ATS*, Chapter I).

The goodness of a set of analytical hypotheses thus turns on more than its predictive utility and fit with the determinable set of dispositions to observable speech behavior. The test of a set of analytical hypotheses is, like the test of any empirical theory, its *explanatory* adequacy. If one set of analytical hypotheses provides a better explanation of the phenomena encompassed by Quine's *limited* empiricism than another, we have *inter alia* a good empirical reason to believe that the term translations which it projects are true of the native language, just as the explanatory power of the kinetic theory of gases gives us good empirical reason to accept it as *descriptively* adequate – i.e., to conclude that *there are* molecules. Quine's bland assurance that two incompatible term translations of, say, 'gavagai', could both "doubtless be accommodated by compensatory variations in analytical hypotheses concerning other locutions" (*W&O*, 72) does not constitute an *argument* for the contrary position.[6]

I argued, first, that Quine's thesis of the indeterminacy of translation and its application as the thesis of the inscrutability of reference were self-defeating. And, indeed, they are. But I have now penetrated more deeply into the foundations of the Quinean positions and have seen them to rest on two complementary misunderstandings. The first of these is a form of verification principle; the second, an inadequate conception of scientific methodology. What makes this of more than parochial interest is that these two misunderstandings form the basis also of instrumentalism as a philosophy of natural science. By assimilating Quine's translation enterprise to the general epistemological model of physical science, then, we are able to see more clearly the roots of the inadequacy of both forms of instrumentalism.

Against this assimilation may be urged what are *genuinely* disanalogies between a linguistic and a physical subject matter. One of these is the *exhaustibility* of linguistic data. The last speaker of Etruscan is long dead, and some day the last extant Etruscan inscription will be uncovered as well, if it has not already been. The set of possible relevant observations, then, will be – if it is not already – closed. And the data we have may well be forever inadequate to determine even the crudest translation of Etruscan into, say, English. Gases, by contrast, endure, and if we, centuries from now, wish to put a new hypothesis to the test, we can be assured of having on hand the phenomena which we need to observe.

The thing to do about this sort of disanalogy is to admit it, but not be dismayed. For the would-be translators of Etruscan are no worse off than the paleontological biologist who would like to say something about, for example, the reproductive habits or coloration of *tyrannosaurus rex*. What is extinct is extinct, and that's the end of the matter. But this is a *de facto* unavailability of evidence, and not an *in principle* one. There is nothing in the nature of a language *as such* which precludes translation, just as there is nothing in the nature of a biological species *as such* which precludes an understanding of its reproductive habits. And just as apparently unrelated discoveries in collateral sciences can have unexpected bearing on outstanding biological questions (thus, for example, radio-carbon dating on the question of the lifespans of members of extinct species) and contemporary reptilian species can illuminate puzzles concerning extinct ones, so there is no way of ruling out *a priori* the possibility that discoveries in collateral sciences and a growing understanding of the way in which languages evolve from one another will some day provide, as well, a key to Etruscan and its dead kindred.

A second, and more critical, disanalogy is the apparently unavoidable use in the translation process of some form of the Principle of Charity – the injunction to so translate our subjects' language that the majority of their utterances are mapped onto domestic *truths*. There are, in other words, truths expressed *in* the target language as well as translational truths *about* it, and the enterprise of translation involves a delicate balancing of the one against the other. I grant this disanalogy with physical inquiry as well. As in the preceding case, I shall remain sanguine about it. But here the issue is more complicated. In fact, it cannot be properly engaged until I have widened my epistemological stage to the point that it includes the rudiments of a theory of empirical truth as well. And this will be my project in the next chapter. There, too, I will begin to have an answer to the question which provided my initial impetus – how does language make representational contact with the world?

CHAPTER V

EXPLANATION AND TRUTH

In the preceding chapter, I isolated certain conceptual features of the process of theory succession in the physical sciences. I argued there that the key to understanding the relationship between a predecessor theory and its successor lay in the notion of *explanation*, for the critical test of a successor theory lay in its explanatory strength. In particular, I argued, there is a constraint on any proposed successor theory for a range of phenomena: that its adoption put us in the position of being able to offer explanatory accounts both of the descriptive successes and of some of the descriptive failures (limit conditions) of its predecessor(s). Once this was seen, it became clear, too, that prediction was methodologically ancillary, serving the function of mapping the explanatory boundaries of a pair of theories and thereby establishing the actual empirical situation to answer to the successor, rather than to the predecessor, descriptions. Thus we could account for the fact that a select handful of predictions can do the total confirmatory job.

The mode of empirical inference centrally constitutive of the scientific method — insofar, at least, as that method is coextensive with the pattern of theory succession in which I have cast it — thus reveals important affinities with what Peirce called *abduction*, the inference to an explanation. On Peirce's original account, abductive inference has the form

> The surprising fact, C, is observed.
> But if A were true, C would be a matter of course.
> Hence there is reason to suspect that A is true. (*A&I*, 151)

If we replace Peirce's psychologistic talk of surprise and suspicion with notions somewhat more precise, the form of reasoning which I have high-lighted in connexion with empirical theory succession may comfortably be recast in accordance with this pattern. In first approximation, it takes the following form:

> The behavior of phenomena is described by laws L of a theory T with a certain degree of accuracy.
> That the actual empirical situation is as described by theory T′ would explain both this behavior of phenomena and some of the limiting conditions of T.

> Hence, there is sufficient reason to adopt T' as a description of the actual empirical situation.

What is important for our present investigations is that this argument purports to be what I shall call a form of *warranting argument*. By this I mean that its conclusion tells us that *there is* a reason for doing something (in this case, for adopting a theory) without exhibiting that reason *as* a reason or even, perhaps, without specifying *what* that reason is. In consequence of these characteristics, a warranting argument, I shall argue, stands midway between a pair of distinct but related arguments of other forms.

The premisses of our warranting argument state that a pair of theories, T and T', stand in a certain relationship. The first of these flanking arguments, then — I shall call it the *first level* argument — is a demonstration that the theories T and T' are related as the premisses claim them to be related, that is, that positing T' as a description of the actual empirical situation *does* enable one to explain both the descriptive successes and some of the descriptive failures of T. This argument, as I have indicated, typically takes the form of a derivation within T', under idealizing assumptions, of *counterparts* to the laws L of T, together with a demonstration that the deviations between the actual situation posited by T' and the idealized situation assumed for the derivation of these counterparts within T' entail failures of fit between the behavior of phenomena described by T' and that posited by T corresponding to at least some of the limiting conditions found to characterize the laws L of T in application.

The conclusion of our warranting argument, on the other hand, is a claim to the effect that, in consequence of the obtaining of this relation between T and T', there is a sufficient reason for adopting T'. But what is it to *adopt* a theory? To answer this question, I shall need to say a bit more than I so far have about the form of a theory and, more generally, about the form of a *law*.

The classical conception of a theory, as I have noted earlier, is that of a set of *generalizations* (hypotheses or laws) sharing a distinctive *theoretical vocabulary*. Notoriously, both of the key terms of this classical characterization have given rise to significant philosophical puzzlements. The central problem concerning generalizations has been the challenge of drawing a distinction between those which are *lawlike* and others thought of as merely adventitious. Traditionally, this issue has taken the form of a debate between defenders of a conception of laws as formulating regularities of co-occurrence and succession among phenomena only and others who perceive laws as possessing a mode of necessity — natural or physical necessity — not

shared by generalizations reporting merely adventitious or coincidental
constant conjunctions of phenomena. Concerning the theoretical
vocabulary, on the other hand, the main problem has been to give an
account of the source and character of its cognitive significance. Here the
positions have ranged from a view of theoretical terms as dispensible, purely
abbreviatory, devices possessing, at best, instrumental significance, to a
stance which regards theoretical terms as possessing meaning-content no less
full-bodied than that which attaches to *de facto* observational terms, often
accompanied by the suggestion that such significance derives from an
"implicit definition" of such terms embodied in the laws constituting the
theory. Yet, like the notion of natural necessity, the notion of implicit
definition has remained unsatisfactorily obscure.

Now the view of empirical theory succession which I have been defending
in the preceding chapter clearly requires that I reject the proposal that
theoretical terms possess instrumental significance only. Yet if a theoretical
vocabulary is supposed to be fully representational, offering a candidate
description of how the world in fact *is*, while at the same time being
adopted in consequence of an explanatory posit, what account can be given
of the significance of theoretical terms?

Interestingly, I have already assembled, in Chapter III, the raw materials
which we need for making some advance on this question. Recall that I
there argued that a term derives its normative identity from its place in a
network of inferential connexions — via *content rules* of inference — to
other terms, rather than through those linguistic responses to non-linguistic
stimuli which constitute language *entries*. Recall, too, that I there explored
a tradeoff between content rules of inference, on the one hand, and unconditionally assertible (analytic) claims on the other, arguing that the latter
should be viewed as object-language counterpart conditionals of the former,
freely assertible because the rules of inference supporting the descriptive
terms which occur essentially in them are *espoused* inferential principles.
What I should now like to suggest is that an exactly parallel set of observations allows us to resolve the traditional puzzles concerning theoretical
terms and natural laws.

What I propose is that we view the laws of a theory as the counterpart
conditionals of a system of *material* rules of inference which, in turn, collectively fix the normative identities of the descriptive theoretical terms
occurring essentially in them and whose uses they govern. *Adopting* a
theory, then, will be acquiring the appropriate reflective dispositions to
draw inferences in accordance with such material rules, and the necessity
attaching to the laws as counterpart conditionals of such material inference

principles will be the unconditional assertibility attaching to the counterpart of any *espoused* rule of inference. To speak here of *natural* (or *physical*) necessity, then, will just be to call attention to the fact that the inference principles supporting the assertion of such generalizations are material, rather than formal, rules of inference, that is, are rules of inference *justified and espoused on empirical (abductive) grounds.*[1]

I shall soon be exploring a family of considerations which further support this view of laws and theories. For now, however, we can observe that, if *adopting* a theory is coming to espouse a variety of material principles of inference, a *reason* for adopting a theory will be a reason for coming to engage in a certain form of inferential conduct. The conclusion of our warranting argument, then, by claiming that a certain fact concerning a pair of theories establishes the existence of such a reason, suggests the availability of yet another argument — I shall call it the *third level* argument — in which the reason itself is *exhibited* as a reason. Since the reason in question is a reason for engaging in a certain form of (inferential) conduct — a reason for *doing* something — the third level argument will be a piece of *practical* reasoning having as its conclusion, roughly, the proximate intention to do what our warranting argument informs us there exists a reason to do — in this case, to adopt T'. The general form of this third level practical argument is, of course, crucial, and will be up for examination shortly.

It is a common tendency, and one to which Peirce succumbs, to take deductive argument as a kind of inferential paradigm. If we do that, then what is called an abductive argument takes on the appearance of a "failed deduction", committing the fallacy of affirming the consequent:

> C (which is surprising)
> But if A, then C (as a matter of course)
> ———————————————
> Therefore, A

If we suppose, then, that abductive argument is a *sui generis* form of argument, in this way on a par with deductive argument, we shall be inclined to cast about for its unique conditions of validity, paralleling the conditions of deductive validity so successfully captured in set theoretic or model theoretic semantics. To see a putative abductive argument as a form of warranting argument, in contrast, is to suppress this inclination. What is called an abductive argument, on this model, is not a special form of argument at all, but rather a second level *schematism*, pointing at a pair of arguments proper — one straightforwardly deductive and the other practical. The critical characteristic of a second level *abductive* schematization (for there are, as we shall soon see, others) is that the reason which its conclusion claims to exist is *identical* to the fact asserted by its premisses to obtain. It is *that* the adoption of T' puts us in the position of being able to explain the successes and failures of T which will function as the credibility-yielding premiss of the third level practical argument, that is, as the *reason for* adopting T'.

The role of an abductive argument, so called, then, is to indicate the availability of a pair of arguments — a first level argument demonstrating, in this case, that the adoption of a certain system of material rules of inference puts us in the position of being able to offer an explanatory account of the descriptive successes and some of the descriptive failures of a predecessor theory, and a third level practical argument in which the fact that we thereby acquire such enhanced explanatory competences itself figures as a reason for actually adopting the appropriate rules of inference. Let me call the credibility attaching to an empirical belief or system of beliefs or to a material rule of inference or system of such rules by virtue of the fact that their acceptance or espousal enhances our *explanatory* competence "abductive credibility". The thesis concerning theory succession for which I have been arguing may then be put succinctly: The credibility of an acceptable successor theory is not instrumental (predictive) but abductive.

The piece of practical reasoning grounding the claim that enhanced explanatory competence *is* a credibility-yielding feature of empirical beliefs or theories (i.e., *is* a reason for their adoption) remains, of course, to be exhibited and defended. Shortly this will be my principal concern. Before doing this, however, I want to broaden and reinforce my conclusion. For, positing for the moment that enhanced explanatory competence is *a* credibility-yielding feature of empirical beliefs or theories, I wish to suggest further that it is, in fact, the *only* such feature. Abductive credibility, in other words, stands at the base, not only of physical theorizing, but of all ampliative inferences and, hence, of empirical knowledge in general.[2]

The central remaining candidate for a form of synthetic (ampliative) inference is some variety of *induction*. I shall thus take my case as basically established if I can argue successfully that the credibility of an acceptable inductive inference is, in fact, also abductive credibility.[3]

The notion of induction is, of course, a polymorphous one. In one of its forms, it is held to be simply the process of the increased predictive confirmation of empirical generalizations posited by the hypothetico-deductive method. But if that is what induction is, then I have already established its essentially abductive character. Or rather, I have argued that there is no such form of empirical inference as that classically held to function in the hypothetico-deductive method. For, first, Duhemian considerations force us to the conclusion that what is being put to the test is not an isolated empirical hypothesis but rather a complex system of empirical posits, any one of which can be held fixed by calling others into question. And, second, credibility does not attach to a system of empirical posits increasingly as the weight of confirmed predictions mounts, but selectively and in quantum jumps as confirmed predictions support the claim that the actual empirical situation answers to the descriptions laid down by the posits.

There is, however, a more venerable picture of induction as *enumerative* or *instantial* induction – an inference from the particular to the general; *inductive generalization*. The standing paradigm of such an inference is something like this:

ARGUMENT I: (The A) a_1 is B
                (The A) a_2 is B
                        .
                        .
                        .
                __(The A) a_n is B__
                Therefore (probably) all A's are B.

Here $a_1, \ldots, a_n$ are objects or phenomena of a certain kind, A, and B is some empirical feature which the premisses assert to be true of each of the objects or phenomena of that kind in our sample. An examination of this paradigm will highlight the essential points to be made about various related versions of inductive inference (e.g., statistical refinements of Argument I) as well.

Before proceeding, however, there is an immediate objection to the paradigm itself which must be met. Argument I, the objection runs, is radically incomplete as I have schematized it. It is not a full inductive argument, but rather an inductive *enthymeme*. What needs to be added is a premiss concerning the character of our *sample* $\Sigma_A = \{a_1, \ldots, a_n\}$ of A's. We require a further premiss asserting that Σ_A consists of *all the observed A's* or is a *random* or *representative* sample of A's.

Now this point is both well and ill taken. It is well taken if it is meant simply to call attention to the fact that the character of our sample will figure crucially in the acceptability of Argument I. But it is ill taken if it is meant as the literal insistence that some specification of the character of the sample be included among the premisses of Argument I. For what specification will do? We may agree, of course, that Argument I will be a *good* inductive argument if and only if Σ_A is a *representative* sample of the A's. But this is not because Σ_A's being representative is a *condition* of the goodness of Argument I. It is rather because Σ_A's being representative is a *consequence* of Argument I's being a good inductive argument *as it stands*. More precisely, to say that Σ_A is a representative sample just *is* to say that Argument I is good as it stands, for a representative sample just *is* one which mirrors the distribution of the property B in the entire reference class of A's, and what we know about the distribution of B in the class of A's we know, if at all, only *through* Argument I. We cannot, therefore, require that Σ_A be known to be representative as a *condition* of conducting Argument I at all.

On the other hand, to say that Σ_A is an *exhaustive* sample of A's or a *random* sample of A's[4] adds not the least credibility to the conclusion of Argument I unless we are in possession of some independent ground for supposing that an exhaustive or a random sample of A's *will be representative*. But, as we shall shortly see, it is precisely Argument I itself – again, as it stands – which alone could provide the kind of ground which we require.

I shall proceed, then, on the assumption that Argument I is, as it stands, the complete schema of an inductive argument. The first thing to note about it is that the 'probably' rider occurring parenthetically in its conclusion is functioning as a commentary on the argument as a whole, much as the rider 'necessarily' in the conclusion of

> If it's raining, then the streets are wet.
> It's raining.
> Therefore, (necessarily) the streets are wet.

signals the fact that this argument is intended to be deductively valid. The necessity in question here is a *relative* necessity. It is not being categorically asserted that *it is necessary that* the streets are wet. Rather it is being claimed that the conclusion "The streets are wet" *follows necessarily from* (is necessary relative to) the premisses. Similarly, the conclusion of Argument I is not the assertion of a categorical probability statement: "It is probable that all A's are B". Rather it is being claimed that the categorial conclusion "All A's are B" *follows inductively from* (is probable relative to) the premisses of the argument. The rider 'probably' serves to indicate (signal) that the categorical conclusion "All A's are B" derives *inductive credibility* from the premisses. It thus has essentially the sense of "It is reasonable to believe, on inductive grounds, all things considered that...". But what are inductive grounds and what is inductive credibility?

Well, to answer that question, what we need to notice is that Argument I has *also* emerged as a putative warranting argument. Its conclusion is also to the effect that there exist good and sufficient reasons for adopting a certain empirical claim. Drawing on my earlier remarks concerning warranting arguments, then, I conclude, first, that the putative inductive argument, Argument I — like the putative abductive argument examined earlier — is not (as it has been represented since Hume) a "failed deduction", possessing its own unique conditions of validity. It is, rather, a second level schematization. As such, it too points to the availability of a pair of further arguments — one first level and deductive, the other third level and practical. But, and this is a critical difference, unlike an explicitly abductive schematization, a (second level) *inductive* schematization does *not* specify in its premises *what* the credibility-yielding feature appealed to as a reason in the third level practical argument is to be. While an abductive schematization indicates the availability of a third level practical argument and specifies the credibility-yielding feature which will figure as a reason in that third level argument, the inductive schematization *merely* indicates the availability of a third level practical argument *without*, however, giving us the raw materials from which such an argument can be constructed.

What I wish to propose is that the credibility of a good inductive argument is, like that of an acceptable successor theory, *abductive* credibility. What warrants the adoption of the conclusion of Argument I is the fact that, by adopting it, we enhance our explanatory competence. We put ourselves, in other words, in the position of being able to offer an explanatory account of something otherwise lacking an explanation. But what is it which gets explained?

It is at *this* point that an appeal to the character of our sample Σ_A becomes apposite. What the acceptance of "All A's are B" enables us to explain is *why only B A's are to be found in our sample*. It forms the fundamentum, in other words, of an explanatory account of the *observed composition* of our sample Σ_A. We can, in fact, recast the inductive warranting argument along the lines of a Peircean abduction. The "surprising fact" of such an abduction will be that we have selected a random or an exhaustive sample of A's (or, more generally, that we have selected a sample of A's according to a specific statistical sampling *technique*, τ) and arrived thereby at a set of objects or phenomena *all of which are B*. The corresponding abductive schematization thus takes the form:

A sample Σ_A of A's selected in accordance with statistical sampling technique τ consists entirely of A's which are B.

That the distribution of B in the entire class of A's is as described by the conclusion of Argument I would explain this composition of Σ_A.

Hence, there is sufficient reason to adopt the conclusion of Argument I as a description of the composition with respect to the feature B of the total class of A's.

The corresponding *first* level argument, then, will be a demonstration of the second premiss of this abductive schematization, a demonstration that, *if* the distribution of the property B in the entire class of A's *is* as described by the conclusion of Argument I, a sample selected in accordance with technique τ will exhibit the distribution observed in Σ_A. If the property B is posited, as it is by the conclusion of Argument I, to be universal in the reference class of A's, then the appeal to the sampling technique τ is, of course, idle, for any sample will, *a fortiori*, be a representative sample. This special case is a crucially important one, and I shall have more to say about it in a moment. For now, however, we should note that the case of a property universal in the reference population is essentially a *limiting* case ($r/s = 1$) of inferences having premisses asserting a property to occur in a sample with *some* relative frequency, r/s, and that, except in such limiting cases, an appeal to the *specific assumptions and constraints* of the sampling technique τ will figure essentially in the demonstration that, given that the relative frequency of the property B in the entire class of A's is r/s, a sample selected in accordance with the technique τ will be representative.

To see more clearly what I am about, it may be useful to observe that the notion of a *representative* sample is a relative of such notions as a *normal* color perceiver and *standard* conditions of perception. A normal color perceiver is − analytically, and from within, as it were − one to whom objects in standard conditions *appear to be* the colors which they in fact *are*. Similarly, standard conditions of (color) perception are − again, analytically − those conditions in which objects appear to normal perceivers to be the colors which they in fact are. The notions of actual color, apparent color, normal perceivers, and standard conditions thus form a cluster, each being exponible within that cluster by its inferential connexions to all of the others. From without, however, the notions of normality of perceivers and standardness of conditions have the epistemological status of *defeasibility* concepts. We discover a variety of specifiable ways in which perceivers may *fail* of normality or conditions *fail* to be standard, that is, an open-ended variety of specifiable empirical circumstances which may be appealed to in offering explanatory accounts of aberrant perceptual behavior.

Analogously, the notion of a representative sample clusters inferentially with the notions of a reliable sampling technique, the observed property distribution in a sample, and the actual property distribution in the entire reference class. A sample is representative if and only if the observed property distribution in the sample is identical to the actual property distribution in the reference class, and a sampling technique is reliable if and only if its application to a population yields samples which are representative. From without, however, the notions of representativeness and reliability again assume the status of defeasibility concepts. We *discover* a variety of specifiable ways in which a sample may fail of representativeness or a sampling technique may fail of reliability, that is, a variety of specifiable empirical circumstances which may be appealed to in offering explanatory accounts of aberrant statistical outcomes.

The first level correlate of an inductive warranting argument trades on just these features of statistical reasoning. For what such a first level argument establishes, if successful, is that the adoption of the conclusion of a second level inductive schematization puts us in the position of being able to explain the descriptive success of our sampling technique, that is, to explain the fact that a sample Σ_A selected in accordance with technique τ *is* representative. In fact, if τ is a *refinement* of a prior sampling technique τ^* which, in application, yielded results concerning the property distribution of B in the class of A's *different* from that exhibited by Σ_A and now imputed to the entire reference class, the parallel with theory succession becomes a complete one. For now we have both the descriptive successes and the descriptive *failures* of τ^* standing in need of an explanatory account. The specific empirical constraints placed on τ^* to yield τ, then, play an explanatory role which is just the converse of that played by the idealizing assumptions appealed to in the reconstruction of a counterpart to a theory T in a successor theory T'. The *failure* of those idealizing assumptions to be descriptively true of the actual empirical situation posited by T' explains the descriptive failures of T. Similarly, the failure of those empirical constraints on sampling to be observed in the *application* of τ^* explains the descriptive failures of τ^*, that is, the failure of τ^* to yield samples representative of the actual distribution of B in the class of A's posited by the conclusion of our inductive schematization.

What I am suggesting, interestingly enough, is this: that *statistical* inductive inference is, logically and epistemologically, theory succession, but *what* the theories in question are theories *of* is statistical sampling. It is the sampling techniques τ and τ^* which play the epistemological roles played in a case of postulational theory formation by the successor and predecessor theories T' and T.

What I have been referring to as empirical constraints on the application of a statistical sampling technique, τ, typically take the form of controlling for disturbing empirical features $F_1, \ldots, F_m$ in the presence of which an A will *not* be B. Another way of representing these empirical constraints (experimental controls), then, will be as a successive *narrowing of the reference class*, from that of all the A's to that of all the A's which are neither F_1 nor F_2 nor... F_m. Looked at in this light, successively refined statistical inferences over a *total* reference class can be seen as *aimed at* a *non-statistical* inductive inference over a *restricted* reference class, an inductive inference, in other words, whose conclusion will posit the property B as being *universal* in the (now narrowed) reference population. The conviction that such a conclusion is always, at least in principle, available is exactly the conviction that there are no irreducibly statistical laws of nature (and the precise sense of Einstein's famous remark "*Gott würfelt nicht.*"). I say "at least in principle" to highlight the fact that the statistical character of an inductive conclusion can frequently be eliminated only by radically reconceiving the initial reference population in terms of a *wholly new* set of descriptive parameters. Perhaps the clearest example of this sort of shift can be found in the reconceiving of statistical nuclear properties of chemical *elements* as averagings of wholly non-statistical nuclear properties of *isotopes*.

Universal, non-statistical, laws may thus be viewed as the target of inductive inference generally. There is a perfectly good reason why this should be the case. It is not simply that, having arrived at a good inductive schematization the conclusion of which (like the conclusion of Argument I) claims a certain property to be universal in a reference class, any appeal to the specific sampling technique drops out as idle. That, of course, is so, for, since all samples will be representative, any sampling technique will do. But the point cuts much deeper. It is only when we are in the possession of a good inductive schematization with *universal* conclusion that we are in a position to explain *the truth of the observational premises* of the schematization. Here, however, we must proceed with some care.

There is surely a temptation, in considering Argument I, to say that the truth of the conclusion of Argument I explains the truth of each of its observational premises. But this way of viewing the matter is, I believe, a serious mistake. It is motivated, of course, by the Hempelian identification of explanation with deduction. Now it is the case that, where we take it as given that a_i is an A, for each i, the truth of "All A's are B" entails the truth of "a_i is B" for each i. But this no more *explains* the fact that, say, a_3 is B than the fact (to adopt an example of Kneale's, *P&I*, 91) that there are two lions in my garden explains the fact that there is at least one lion in my garden, although the former fact does entail the latter.

What may lead us to think that the truth of "All A's are B" explains the truth of, say, "a_3 is B" is the fact that acceptance of the conclusion of Argument I does *put us in the position* to offer an explanatory account of the truth of "a_3 is B". But, and here is where we make contact with my earlier remarks regarding the form of a law, it does this *only* if we interpret the conclusion as the counterpart conditional of a material rule of inference positing a necessary connexion between being an A and being B. In the explanation of the fact that a_3 is B, in other words, the conclusion of Argument I does not play a premissory role but rather an inference-warranting role. It is not the fact that all A's are B which explains the fact that a_3 is B. Rather it is the fact *that a_3 is an A* which explains this. The explanation of the fact that a_3 is B, in other words, takes the form:

ARGUMENT II: $\underline{\quad a_3 \text{ is an A}\quad}$
Therefore, (necessarily) a_3 is B.

The necessity in question here is, of course, natural necessity and, as I noted earlier, to speak here of natural necessity is just to say that the principle which licenses the inference of the conclusion of Argument II from its premiss is a *material*, rather than a formal, rule of inference, that is, a rule of inference justified and adopted on empirical grounds.

What I am proposing, in other words, is that we look at an inductive schematization with *universal* conclusion as indicating the availability of a third level practical argument supporting the adopting of a material rule of inference corresponding to that conclusion. The reason for adopting this inferential policy, appealed to in this third level argument, will be precisely that, by doing so, we put ourselves in a position to offer explanatory accounts of the truth of each of the observational premisses of the original schematization. The credibility attaching to the conclusion of an inductive schematization is thus, again, *abductive* credibility, an enhancement of our ability to give explanatory accounts of particular empirical occurrences or phenomena. And the form of one of these newly possible explanatory accounts will be precisely that given by Argument II.

The warrant for construing Argument II as the *complete* model for such an explanatory account parallels the argument given in Chapter III for the non-derivative authority of *content* rules of inference. If one attempts to construe Argument II as an enthymeme, having the conclusion of Argument I as a suppressed *premiss*, one runs up against precisely the ambiguity of the conditional which I discussed earlier. The conclusion of Argument I must surely be strong enough to warrant the assertion of "If c_1 *were* an A, then c_1 *would* be B". For if it were not – if, that is, the conclusion of Argument I did not purport to establish a necessary connexion between being an A and being B — then Argument II would surely be devoid of explanatory force. We would then be back in the situation of explaining the presence of at least one lion by appealing to the presence of two or, to vary the example, of explaining the fact that a beveled mirror shows spectra in sunlight by remarking that all beveled mirrors do this. (Hanson, *ILSD*, 30.) If it does not follow, in *some* interesting sense of 'follow', from the fact that a_3 is an A that it is B, then the fact that a_3 is an A cannot be even a significant part of what *explains* why a_3 is B.[5]

I conclude, then, that accepting the conclusion of Argument I is coming to espouse a material rule of inference. And the grounds for adopting this material inference principle are, I have argued, *abductive*. We adopt it precisely because, by doing so, we put ourselves in the position of being able to offer *explanatory* accounts of the truth of the observational premises of Argument I, that is, we enhance our explanatory competence.

Let me collect some results. The view of empirical reasoning in general which I have been defending holds, briefly, that coming to accept empirical generalizations and coming to adopt empirical theories is coming to espouse material inference principles or, in the case of theories, *systems* of material rules of inference. These material rules of inference are adopted on *abductive* grounds — on the grounds, that is, that their espousal places us in the position of being able to offer explanatory accounts of, in the one case, particular empirical phenomena and, in the other, *in addition*, the descriptive successes and failures of predecessor theories.

I stress, in the case of theories, "in addition", because the link between postulational theory and observational phenomena is not *essentially* mediated by pure observational generalizations of the classical inductive sort, however well-supported they may be by the theoretical structure. Rather, a postulational theory purports to give a description of the actual empirical situation, and thus admits of the redescription of observational phenomena in the theoretical language *directly* as instantiations of theoretical parameters or instances of theoretical kinds. To call an entity a "theoretical entity", on this view, is thus not to attenuate its ontological status. Rather it is to identify it as an entity knowledge of which is obtained by *theoretical reasoning* — i.e., by postulational abductive reasoning.

If all of this is so far correct, we obtain a picture of scientific progress as the building up through time of a system of material inference rules of increasing explanatory power. The resulting *material* inferential structure parallels the structure of *content* rules which I argued in Chapter III is constitutive of a natural language. In fact, I believe, we have here more than a parallel, for, I shall argue, the two structures are, in the end, one. Furthermore, not only are material rules and content rules to be identified with each other, but, in addition, they will be identified in turn with rules of *truth* for empirical claims. But before this argument can be successfully carried through, a few more pieces must be assembled.

The first of these is the extension of the notion of a language entry to the theoretical context. The inferential structure of content rules established in Chapter III admitted of entries on the model of conceptual responses to non-conceptual stimuli. The behavior-shaping constitutive of language learning established responses of two different sorts — the language-language responses which were inference and the world-language responses which were perceptual entries. Applied to the current question, this standpoint treats the inferential structure of material rules constitutive of a physical theory as a structure admitting perceptual entries on the same model. Observationality, on this account, is thus a *de facto* property of an empirical claim rather than an essential one. What we have here is something quite like Feyerabend's pragmatic theory of observation (*ERE*). There are no *logical* reasons, in other words, for rejecting the possibility that the structure of theoretical concepts be entered *directly*, rather than by making an inferential stop at a bridge law, translation rule, or correspondence rule. All that is needed is that the theorizers be so trained that they respond to non-linguistic stimuli with claims framed in the theoretical idioms and carrying the full theoretical conceptual load. And for such a claim to "carry the full theoretical conceptual load" just is for the theorizer actively to espouse (i.e., in first approximation, to be so trained as to be disposed to act inferentially in accord with) the system of material rules of inference constitutive of the theory thus entered.[6]

The structure of content rules and perceptual language-entries developed in Chapter III thus exhibits a strong analogy with the structure of material rules and perceptual theory-entries which I have been developing in this chapter. To make this more than a strong analogy, however, it is necessary to explore the logic of a term which has so far served largely as a crucial unexplicated parameter of my reasoning. Specifically, we must ask what an *explanation* is and in virtue of what an argument comes to have an explanatory force. If I have been correct in my (schematic) argument that abductive credibility is the sole support of ampliative (empirical) reasoning, we can hardly expect to make any further progress until we have done so.

What, then, is an explanation? The first point is that there is an analytic connexion between the notions of explanation and *understanding*. What we understand and what we can explain are not just contingently coextensive. The process of coming to explain a range of phenomena *is* the process of coming to understand them. We understand *only* what we can explain. That this is so may be reinforced by the observation that, at a given time, not everything stands in *need* of explanation. This is an essentially synchronic remark, for what is held fixed and not demanding explanation at one time may well be up for an explanatory account at a later date. To stand in need of explanation, a phenomenon must typically be seen as in some way *anomalous* or *deviant*. This is strikingly highlighted by the fact that any theory carries with it what Toulmin has called (*F&U*) "ideals of natural order" – tacit presumptions as to the *ordinary* course of natural events. Thus within Newton's Theory, for example, it is *accelerated* motions which stand in need of explanation, and this is so because they are seen as deviations from the *natural* tendency of objects to exhibit uniform rectilinear motion. That an object at rest or exhibiting uniform rectilinear motion continues to do so, however, is not *explained* by Newton's Theory. Rather, it is one of the theory's *posits*.

What stands in need of an explanation at a given time, then, is what is deviant or anomalous, what then fails to cohere with our then-current understanding of the natural order. I propose, consequently, that we take as the *root* notion of explanation *the achieving of a coherent understanding*. Under this rubric will fall not only explanations in natural science but explanations in the social sciences and, indeed, in everyday life as well. We have explained a phenomenon, then, when we have found a place for it in a preexisting conceptual structure or, failing that, when we have so modified the preexisting conceptual structure as to produce an enriched structure in which the formerly anomalous phenomenon has a place.

Explanation thus emerges, not as deduction, but as *redescription*. We explain Keplerian orbital motion and Galilean fee-fall by redescribing them as accelerated (Newtonian) motions under the primary determinant of a central gravitational force. We explain the classical macro-behavior of gases by redescribing it as the behavior of ensembles of micro-particles. And we explain, for example, the spread of disease by redescribing it as the transmittal of living micro-organisms from one host organism to another. The end-in-view in each case is the same, to give the phenomena so redescribed a place in a unified conceptual structure constituted and lent coherence by a set of material rules of inference – to achieve a coherent understanding.

What I want next to suggest is that this notion of achieving a coherent understanding is precisely what Peirce had in mind when he spoke of the *fixation of belief*. I have spoken of phenomena seen as deviant or anomalous, as standing in need of explanation. Peirce speaks of doubt, "an uneasy and dissatisfied state from which we struggle to free ourselves and pass into the state of belief." (*FB*, 10) 'Belief', for Peirce, has a pragmatic (behavioral) import.

The feeling of believing is a more or less sure indication of there being established in our nature some habit which will determine our actions. (*FB*, 10)

Peirce represents inquiry as arising from the irritation of doubt and terminating in the settlement of opinion or fixation of belief. The picture which I have presented is fully analogous to this. It represents empirical inquiry as the continuing effort to integrate deviant or anomalous phenomena into a unified coherent conceptual structure. This structure is constituted, on my picture, by a set of material rules of inference, which, like Peirce's 'belief', have behavioral consequences. Espousal of a material rule is, in first approximation, a (reflective) behavioral disposition to proceed from position to position within a language game in which positions are claims.

The argument of "The Fixation of Belief" is, in essence, a piece of practical reasoning, concerned with the means of achieving a given end. The end, in this case, is epistemic – the achieving of settled opinion (in my terms, a maximally coherent understanding), and the question of means is the question of what methodological policy to adopt best to serve this end. Structurally, the argument may be schematized thus:

(1)   We shall achieve a specific end E.
(2)   The best (or only) way of achieving E is by adopting a methodological policy of kind K.
(3)   The specific methodological policy SM is of kind K.

Hence,   ―――――――――――――

(4)   We shall adopt the policy SM.

Here E is the end of fixing belief, and premiss (1) is to be viewed as an expression of our standing *intention* to achieve that end (an intention which itself will be up for scrutiny in a later chapter). SM, of course, is the method of science, and the conclusion, (4), functions as the expression of a derivative, proximate intention to adopt beliefs as they satisfy the methodological tenets of scientific inquiry. The bulk of the argument in Peirce's essay is devoted to establishing a characterization, K, of the constraints on a methodological policy adequate to the achieving of the expressed end-in-view. His *method* is to consider a variety of alternative methodological policies and, by identifying the ways in which each *fails* to achieve the professed end, to isolate the necessary constraints on any adequate (success-ful) policy.

The first of these inadequate methods Peirce calls "the method of tenacity". It consists in

... taking as answer to a question any we may fancy, and constantly reiterating it to ourselves, dwelling on all which may conduce to that belief, and learning to turn with contempt and hatred from anything that might disturb it. (*FB*, 11)

The method of tenacity, however, is inherently unstable. In practice, it will necessarily fail to settle opinion.

The man who adopts it will find that other men think differently from him, and it will be apt to occur to him, in some saner moment, that their opinions are quite as good as his own, and this will shake his confidence in his belief. (*FB*, 12)

A methodological policy adequate for fixing belief must thus be *inter-personal* – suitable for fixing belief in a *community* of inquirers and not simply for an individual in isolation.

Hence, the second method Peirce considers is the "method of *authority*". Here the will of the state or church replaces the will of the individual and regulates opinion collectively for the community.

Let an institution be created which shall have for its object to keep correct doctrines before the attention of the people, to reiterate them perpetually, and to teach them to the young; having at the same time power to prevent contrary doctrines from being taught, advocated, or expressed. (*FB*, 13)

The method of authority, too, will fail, however, in the first instance because it lacks *universal scope*: "...no institution can undertake to regulate opinions upon every subject". (*FB*, 14) Consequently, men will in time come to

... see that men in other countries and in other ages have held to very different doctrines from those which they themselves have been brought up to believe; and they cannot help seeing that it is the mere accident of their having been taught as they have, and of their having been surrounded with the manners and associations they have, that has caused them to believe as they do and not far differently. (*FB*, 14)

The method of authority thus fails to be sufficiently *a-cultural* and *a-temporal* in its application. What is needed is a method which will "not only produce an impulse to believe, but shall also decide what proposition it is which is to be believed." (*FB*, 15) That is, the *method* must yield the *belief* as well as the believing of it. Only in this way can the personal, temporal, and cultural influences which vitiated the methods of tenacity and authority be avoided.

The third method considered by Peirce, the *a priori* method, initially commends itself on these grounds. Here

... the action of natural preferences [is] unimpeded,... and under their influence... men, conversing together and regarding matters in different lights, gradually develop beliefs in harmony with natural causes. (*FB*, 15)

The *a priori* method, however, does not differ in essence from the method of authority, Peirce argues, and fails of adequacy on the same sort of grounds.

The government may not have lifted its finger to influence my convictions; I may have been left outwardly quite free to choose... But... I cannot help seeing that, though governments do not interfere, sentiments in their development will be very greatly determined by accidental causes. (*FB*, 17–8)

The *a priori* method

... makes of inquiry something similar to the development of taste; but taste, unfortunately, is always more or less a matter of fashion... (*FB*, 16–7)

The *a priori* method thus fails too, in the end, to be sufficiently a-temporal and a-cultural. The only way of guaranteeing in fact that these constraints are met, Peirce concludes, is by establishing a method

... by which our beliefs may be determined by nothing human, but by some external permanency – by something upon which our thinking has no effect.

Our external permanency... must be something which affects, or might affect, every man. And, though these affections are necessarily as various as are individual conditions, yet the method must be such that the ultimate conclusion of every man shall be the same. (*FB*, 18)

An adequate method, thus, must be not only inter-personal but *impersonal*. It must *admit of a right and wrong* in application, and must be *self-corrective* in order that the opinions of various differently situated inquirers may *converge* to a common conception.

Collating these results leads Peirce to the desired characterization, K, of the sought methodological policy. Any method adequate for the settlement of opinion or fixation of belief must be inter-personal, a-cultural, a-temporal, impersonal, of universal scope, self-corrective, and convergent. It is the method of science alone which satisfies this characterization.

The scientific method is, as I have schematized it, the method of abductive reasoning – the inference to an explanation. It is, in essence, *tailored* to fulfill the end of attaining maximally coherent understanding, for it takes as the *test* of the acceptability of an empirical claim its contribution to the increasing coherence of understanding. No empirical phenomena are *a priori* excluded from the scope of scientific theorizing, and the method qualifies, too, on the critical ground of impersonality, for it is the world which yields up deviant or anomalous phenomena to be conceptually integrated into our prior understanding, and while an explanatory hypothesis is, to be sure, a free human creation, the question of whether or not such an hypothesis *successfully explains* what it is offered to explain is not, similarly, a matter of arbitrary decision or inclination.

Now it may be objected here that in taking the aim of the enterprise of inquiry to be, with Peirce, the achieving of a maximally coherent understanding, I have radically falsified the essential character of that enterprise. For surely, it will be said, the epistemic end controlling the scientific enterprise must be nothing less than the possession of empirical *truth*. The aim must surely be, not merely the possession of maximally coherent explanatory accounts, but the possession of *explanations*, i.e., of *true* explanatory accounts. Peirce's reply at this point is instructive:

> We may fancy that this is not enough for us, and that we seek, not merely an opinion, but a true opinion. But put this fancy to the test, and it proves groundless; for as soon as a firm belief is reached we are entirely satisfied, whether the belief be true or false. And it is clear that nothing out of the sphere of our knowledge can be our object, for nothing which does not affect the mind can be the motive for mental effort. The most that can be maintained is, that we seek for a belief that we shall *think* to be true. But we think each one of our beliefs to be true, and, indeed, it is mere tautology to say so. (*FB*, 10–1)

The point here made is essentially a negative one. It is that the epistemic ends-in-view controlling the enterprise of empirical inquiry must be the sort of things that can be *known to be realized*, be known to obtain. Now a true belief differs from a false belief *not intrinsically* but rather in its *relation* to the "external permanency", to the world. And this is the point of Peirce's remark that "nothing which does not affect the mind can be the motive for mental effort". That a belief be accepted only if it is true cannot be part of our *methodological* canons. Empirical beliefs are essentially defeasible. To suppose that they are not is once again to eschew impersonality of method, for there can be no *a priori* guarantee that the course of future events will not be such as to yield anomalies to *any* prior structure of conceptions. But, if this is so, then that we are, at a given time, in final possession of empirical truth cannot be known. And if it cannot be known, it cannot serve as a methodological constraint on the process of empirical inquiry. We can, of course, *believe* ourselves to be in possession of empirical truth, but, as Peirce points out, *whatever* we believe we believe to be true, and this, then, cannot function as a *constraint* on a methodological policy for fixing *what* to believe.

But, on the positive side, while Peirce recognizes that the possession of empirical truth cannot be an aim *controlling* the enterprise of scientific inquiry, he holds, too, that the scientific enterprise *issues in* empirical truth — and that itself is a necessary truth. For Peirce, (ideal) empirical truth just *is* the ideal or limiting outcome of the process of scientific inquiry.

One man may investigate the velocity of light by studying the transits of Venus and the abberation of the stars; another by the oppositions of Mars and the eclipses of Jupiter's satellites; a third by the method of Fizeau; a fourth by that of Foucault; a fifth by the motions of the curves of Lissajoux; a sixth, a seventh, an eighth, and a ninth, may follow the different methods of comparing the measures of statical and dynamical electricity. They may at first obtain different results, but, as each perfects his method and his processes, the results are found to move steadily together toward a destined center. So with all scientific research.

The opinion which is fated to be ultimately agreed to by all who investigate, is what we mean by truth, and the object represented in this opinion is the real. That is the way I would explain reality. (*HMIC*, 38)

Peirce, then, not only identifies material rules of inference with content rules[7] but with the rules of truth for the representations which they ground as well. Ideal empirical truth is identified with assertibility in accordance with the principles of the limiting theoretical outcome of scientific inquiry. And, correlatively, we may identify truth here-and-now (i.e., the epistemologically best-grounded answer to the question of what, here and now, we can truly say about the world) with assertibility in accordance with the principles of the *current* theoretical outcome of scientific inquiry. Empirical truth in general, then, will be assertibility in accordance with the material rules of explanatory theory (employing, of course, whatever collateral considerations the rules themselves demand that we impose).[8]

Now this conception of truth has been objected to on a variety of grounds. Perhaps the central argument is that encapsulated in this passage from Quine:

Peirce was tempted to define truth outright in terms of scientific method, as the ideal theory which is approached as a limit when the (supposed) canons of scientific method are used unceasingly on continuing experience. But there is a lot wrong with Peirce's notion, besides its assumption of a final organon of scientific method and its appeal to infinite process. There is a faulty use of numerical analogy in speaking of a limit of theories, since the notion of limit depends on that of "nearer than" which is defined for numbers and not for theories. And even if we by-pass such troubles by identifying truth somewhat fancifully with the ideal result of applying scientific method outright to the whole future totality of surface irritations, still there is trouble in the imputation of uniqueness ("*the* ideal result"). For... we have no reason to suppose that man's surface irritations even unto eternity admit of any one systematization that is scientifically better or simpler than all possible others. It seems likelier, if only on account of symmetries or dualities, that countless alternative theories would be tied for first place. (*W&O*, 23)

Several criticisms are to be found in this passage. In the first place, there is the imputation to Peirce of a false belief in a single "final organon of scientific method". Now this is both well and ill-taken. It is well-taken if, by "final organon" Quine means an algorithm for theory-construction – a "logic of discovery" in one traditional sense. There is no *a priori* reason to believe that a set of rules constituting a *discovery procedure* for adequate theoretical postulations can be drawn up in advance of experiential anomalies which give rise to the need for new theoretical posits. Thus, Quine is right to hold that no such final organon can be set down. But he is wrong to hold Peirce committed to its possibility. Peirce's commitments extend only to the isolation of a unique *epistemology* for science – the characterization of the method of science as essentially abductive – and Quine's point in ill-taken if his rejection of a "final organon" is to be interpreted as the rejection of the view that scientific inquiry is controlled by a method establishing *canons of correctness*. There *is* a test for theoretical adequacy; it is the explanatory power of the successor theory *vis-à-vis* its predecessor(s). Only this far is Peirce committed. But that his commitments extend this far already carries him beyond Quine's instrumentalistic stance, for Quine takes the end-in-view of scientific inquiry to be the "systematization" of "surface irritations" and, thus, cannot discriminate among *ad hoc* posits equally successful in their predictive fit – the epicyclic refinements of explanatorily sterile conceptual schemes.

Once the abductive structure of theory confirmation has been laid bare, we have seen too that there is no difficulty concerning imputations of *uniqueness*. For, as I argued in the preceding chapter, the fact that a pair of incompatible competing theories apply over a range of physical phenomena is itself a fact standing in need of explanation and thus becomes the best reason we *could* have for believing that the theoretical task is not at an end.

More troublesome, however, is Quine's argument that "the notion of limit depends on that of 'nearer than' which is defined for numbers and not for theories". And the problem here is exacerbated when we realize that the limiting theory, *being* a limit, is not conceptually accessible to us here-and-now, nor, indeed, at any *actual* stage of scientific inquiry. How, then, are we to make some *non-metaphorical* sense of the notion of theoretical convergence?

The thing to do in this case is to grant Quine's point that 'nearer than' is defined in the first instance for numbers and not for theories. But the *caveat* "in the first instance" is crucial. For theories generate numbers. The conceptual apparatus of pure mathematics (and logic) is *theory-neutral.* (That is what makes it *pure* or *formal*, surely.) It is common to predecessor and successor theory alike. Now I have argued that the prime constraint on a successor theory is that it explain the descriptive successes and some of the descriptive failures (limiting conditions) of its predecessor(s), and, further, that such explanation is in essence *redescription* of the old theoretical parameters and phenomena in the conceptual setting of the new theory. More precisely, the successor theory must explain why phenomena obey the laws of the predecessor(s) to the extent that they have been found to do so. And, I argued, the way in which this comes about is that the successor theory posits an actual empirical situation and a set of laws governing it in a way which admits the *modeling* of the predecessor parameters and laws within the new theory. The explanation of predecessor descriptive successes is achieved, then, by establishing that the empirical situation posited by the predecessor theory is a *close approximation* to what the successor theory now posits as the actual empirical situation. And here is where the neutral coin of number comes into play. For one can derive the *actual* laws relating the *counterpart* (modeling) concepts of predecessor parameters within the successor theory and compare them with the *models* of the *predecessor* laws within that same successor theory. The successor theory can thus be viewed as introducing a *correction factor* into the (counterpart) laws of its predecessor(s). That correction factor yields absolute numerical values when actual magnitudes of successor theory parameters are supplied. *As these numerical magnitudes converge to 0*, we may say, in a clear and non-metaphorical sense, that *the successive theories are converging to a limit as well.*[9]

It is important to understand just what I have done here. Nothing that I have said impugns the conceptual *incommensurability* of predecessor and successor theories for which Feyerabend has forcefully argued (*PE, PE2*). There need be, and typically is, no *sharing* of descriptive concepts between predecessor and successor theories. What I have argued is only that the prime explanatory constraint on theory succession requires that we be able to *model* the predecessor theory in the successor by means of *counterpart* concepts. Where we find common ground is not in the descriptive content of the various theories but in the neutral currency of mathematics. What converges in the *primary* sense is a sequence of numbers — the absolute numerical magnitudes of the correction factors required to adjust the *counterparts* of predecessor laws within the successor theory to the values derivable from the actual successor laws instantiated to actual values of successor parameters.

I have, too, made no use of a putative extra-theoretical Archimedean standpoint in characterizing this notion of theoretical convergence to a limit. My pattern of reasoning has not been patterned on that of Weierstrass Convergence, where a sequence of numbers — $s_1, \ldots, s_n, \ldots$ — is shown to converge to a *known* numerical limit, s, by establishing that the value of members of the sequence ultimately approximates the limiting value with any arbitrary degree of accuracy:

$$(\epsilon)\,(\exists N)\,(n)\,(n > N \rightarrow |s_n - s| \leqslant \epsilon).$$

Rather it fits more closely the model of *Cauchy* Convergence. Here a sequence of numbers is shown to converge to a numerical limit (not necessarily known) by establishing that the values of members of the sequence ultimately approximate arbitrarily closely *to each other*:[10]

$$(\epsilon)\,(\exists N)\,(m)\,(n)\,(m > N \,\&\, n > N\,.\rightarrow\,.\,|s_n - s_m| \leqslant \epsilon).$$

I remarked earlier that any theory fits any set of data with a certain amount of slack. What I am suggesting now is that theoretical progress is marked by the *decreasing* slack with which successive theories fit *increasingly refined* data. And this can be the case despite the fact that theory succession necessarily involves a (perhaps radical) reconception of that data. Thus theoretical convergence is not a mere metaphor, but rather a notion which can be epistemologically well-founded. It is a derivative convergence, obtaining its confirmation from convergence in the primary and literal sense — the convergence of sequences of numbers.

Let me collect the argument to this point. I have argued that ampliative (empirical) reasoning, whether that of postulational theory formation or that of what is classically termed instantial or enumerative induction, is uniformly and essentially grounded in considerations of abductive credibility, the enhancement of our explanatory competences. Explanation, I suggested, was, in its root sense, the achieving of a coherent understanding. In detail, coherent understanding of phenomena is attained by providing *redescriptions* of the phenomena in terms of which they come to serve as entries to a conceptual structure constituted by a network of material inference principles. These material rules of inference were then identified with the content rules of an empirical descriptive language; language becoming thus in essence theory writ large. Finally these content rules were further identified with rules of empirical truth for claims framed in terms of the concepts which they constitute, and this conception of empirical truth as the ideal outcome of empirical (abductive) methodology was defended against the basic criticisms which it is likely to encounter.

What may at this point be unclear is the relationship of this generalized account of scientific and, more broadly, empirical inquiry to the problems of representation with which I began. Unfortunately, I have still not assembled *all* the pieces needed to settle this question. What can be said at this point is this: I began with a question "How is it possible for language to represent the world?" The question posits two structures — one linguistic and one extra-linguistic — and a semantic relationship between them. In Chapter II, I argued that to come to grips with this question, we must step outside of semantic categories — neither agent-semantics nor its underpinning of mentalistic (intentionalistic) semantics supplies an answer to the original problem of fitting the linguistic to the non-linguistic structure. Rather, such mentalistic gambits provide at best *further structures* for which the question of fit then re-emerges. What I then proceeded to do was to investigate the way in which *one* of these structures — the linguistic — is constituted and *how it evolves under the causal impact of the other.* We now have a view of language as theory writ large — a structure of entries and inferences evolving to higher and higher states of coherence and integration under the continuing impact of anomalous experiential inputs. It is in this *causal evolutionary* conception of word-world relations that the answer to our original puzzle will lie. But before I can bring this conception fully together with the original questions, it is necessary to overcome the gap between word and world by returning to the linguistic phenomena *in extension* — to the realm of natural linguistic objects — and considering the anatomy of a basic claim. Only in this way can we get clear about the *sort* of extensional word-world fitting which is needed to ground the semantic relation of representation which was our initial impetus.

Before doing so, though, a word should be said about the relationship of the picture which I have been sketching to the question of ontological priorities. In taking the realistic view of scientific theories demanded by viewing them as arising out of an abductive methodology, it may seem that I open myself to the possibility of concluding that the world of commonsense middle-sized physical objects and persons is, in some sense, merely phenomenal. And this is so. For I have held that a successor theory purports — and, if it is explanatorily adequate, (synchronically) purports successfully — to delineate the actual empirical situation. If what is thus posited by an explanatorily superior theory is in some sense incompatible with the world view of commonsense, then, it is the world of commonsense which must give ontological ground. There is, consequently, a criterion of ontological priority implicit in this manner of proceeding. What it is can best be brought out by contrasting it with Strawson's.

Strawson grounds ontological priorities in the order of *identification*. Particulars of one type, A, are ontologically prior to particulars of another type, B, if particulars of type B cannot be *identified* without reference to particulars of type A, while no reference to particulars of type B is required to identify particulars of type A. (*I*, 17). Now I have already explored, in Chapter II, the limitations of the Strawsonian notion of identification. What is crucial to the present considerations is the fact that Strawsonian identification, being ultimately grounded in demonstrative identification, is substantively a question of language or theory *entries*. Now earlier I argued in defense of something like Feyerabend's pragmatic theory of observation. Nothing in principle, I claimed, stands in the way of a structure of material or content rules being entered *directly* at *any* point. The application of this observation to the current case is straightforward, for if nothing in the logic of inquiry rules out direct perceptual entries to any point of a theoretical inference-structure, nothing *in principle* stands in the way of "demonstrative identification" of particulars of *any* type. Of course, much may stand in the way of such identifications *in practice*, unaugmented and unaided human perceptual equipment being limited as it is. Such limitations, however, are not logical but methodological. And as such, they cannot ground an ontological priority.

In contrast, the criterion which I implicitly offer may be made explicit thus: Particulars of type A are ontologically prior to particulars of type B if we must appeal to particulars of type A to *explain* what we already know about particulars of type B. Ontological priority is grounded, not in identification priority, but in priority in the order of *explanation*. What supports this criterion is the identification, earlier argued for, of the ideal outcome of abductive methodology with empirical truth. And what, in turn, supports the possible phenomenality of the world of commonsense is the fact that explanation is redescription. If the redescription of type-B particulars in terms of the entities and parameters of the theoretical framework positing type-A particulars is sufficiently radical, then, we may be put in the position of making the well-grounded judgment that, as the explanatory success of our successor theory establishes, the actual empirical situation contains *no* particulars answering to the descriptive posits of our predecessor theory – i.e., *no* particulars of type B at all. And this can, logically, be the case even if the particulars of type B are the middle-sized physical objects and persons of the commonsense world. But we are not cut entirely adrift here. For the constraints on theory succession demand, as I have frequently stressed, that the successor theory be able to explain the descriptive successes of its predecessor(s). It follows then that any conceptual framework purporting to replace the framework of commonsense must explain the descriptive successes of *its* predecessor – and that is, that it must explain why it is that, given that there *are* no commonsense physical objects, it is nevertheless the case that there certainly *appear* to be. Needless to say, no total conceptual structure purporting to adequacy in *this* sense is currently more than *very* schematically in hand.

Finally, I am in a position to make partial payment on my promissory note of the preceding chapter concerning the Principle of Charity. The Principle enjoins, recall, that we so translate our subjects' language that the majority of their utterances are mapped onto domestic *truths*. What we are now in a position to see is that the Principle of Charity, properly understood, is the methodological fallout of a necessary truth – that the majority of empirical claims of a population of language users must be true. And this for the simple reason that the content rules constitutive of their descriptive language *are* the rules of truth for empirical claims couched in that language; that is, that empirical truth *is* assertibility in accordance with the relevant content rules and such collateral considerations as the rules themselves may impose.

The notion of truth at work here is, crucially, *synchronic* here-and-now truth and not the ideal (diachronic) truth to which evolving conceptual structures tend. Thus if the subject population is *too* primitive or *too* advanced, it will in practice be impossible to map their claims onto what are *here-and-now* empirical truths for us. Yet the conceptual structure of this population cannot be *totally* unrelated to our own. For there is, in the end, only *one* empirical methodology – the abductive – and if it is, as it must be, the *same* world which is ultimately shaping the linguistic and conceptual evolution of our target population and ourselves, both their conceptual structure and our own must find a place as stages in a single, directed, evolutionary process converging ultimately toward that *ideal* empirical truth envisioned by Peirce.

Yet this is only a partial payment. For there are deep metaphysical issues at stake here – indeed, realism itself is at stake – and so I shall return to these questions once more, in my final chapter. Foundation before edifice, however. Let me turn once again to the consideration of language proper.

CHAPTER VI

THE PROTOSEMANTIC OF BASIC CLAIMS

By 'protosemantics', I mean the study of vehicles of representation *in extension*, as elements of the natural order. Viewing vehicles of representation as themselves empirical structures, one can say something about their extensional relationships both to one another and to other elements of the natural order which, unlike vehicles of representation, do not *also* admit of pure normative characterizations. And one can provide an ontological parsing or assay of the representing structures themselves. These enterprises collectively constitute what I call 'protosemantics'. Examples should make things clearer.

Let me begin by distinguishing two aspects of *iconic* depiction paralleling the distinction between designation and claiming earlier drawn for languages. These aspects can most readily be highlighted by considering an hypothetical series of political cartoons. These are all cartoons *of* Richard Nixon, but, as political cartoons will, they reflect their creators' differing political persuasions. One represents Nixon as fat and happy; another as lean and hungry. One represents him as an uncanonized saint; another as a fallen angel. One represents him as being compassionate; another as being malicious. Each is a representation *of* him, but each represents him *as* (being) something different from the others. Representation *of* and representation *as* thus parallel designation and claiming. Representation *of* picks out a subject; representation *as* makes a (pictorial) claim about it.

I shall need some terminology to isolate these two aspects of iconic depiction. Let me say that a picture *indicates* what (i.e., the object which) it is a picture *of* and *portrays* that thing as (being) of some kind or character. The correlative functions, then, I shall call 'indication' and 'portrayal'. Thus, for example, one of the series of cartoons indicates Richard Nixon and portrays him as fat and happy. The parallels between indication and designation on the one hand and between portrayal and claiming on the other are, of course, not yet exact. Claiming, for example, goes with that-clauses in a way which has no obvious parallel in the case of portrayal. Now I think that the parallelism can be firmed up, but first I want to understand indication and portrayal more clearly.

Like designation, indication can *prima facie* be both "definite" and "indefinite". For example, I may paint a picture of Richard Nixon – and this is definite indication – or I may simply paint a picture of *a man* – and this is indefinite indication. The latter picture, we may say, indicates a man, just as the former indicates Nixon. The place to begin, I think, is with indefinite indication.

Suppose then that I am painting a picture of *balloons*. The balloons are of different colors. In order to do this, I put down on my canvas Q-shaped patches of pigment in various colors. Each Q-shaped patch indicates a balloon. By being of such-and-such a color, a Q-shaped patch portrays the balloon which it indicates as being of such-and-such a color. Thus, in a standard sort of case, a red Q-shaped patch indicates a balloon and portrays it as being red; a blue Q-shaped patch indicates a balloon and portrays it as being blue; and so on.

Part of what makes this mode of depiction *iconic* is the fact that the colors of the Q-shaped patches indicating balloons and the colors of the balloons which they indicate are the same. Both patch and balloon are red, blue, yellow, or what have you. This is the clearest sense in which a representation can resemble that which it represents. That the patches are Q-shaped contributes to resemblance, too, but here the matter is more complicated, for the balloons indicated are not Q-shaped. One can locate something Q-shaped in the situation, however. The orthogonal 2-dimensional projection of one of the indicated balloons (e.g., the *shadow* of one of the balloons) is Q-shaped. This, too, may be counted as a resemblance between the representation and what it represents. But it is more tenuous than the resemblance in color.

Nor, I think, is there anything *in general* which one can say in advance about what *is* going to count as a resemblance between representation and represented. But this should not give us pause, for, even in the case of iconic depiction, it is not by virtue of any resemblance between representation and represented that the former succeeds in representing the latter. This has been persuasively argued, and at length, by Goodman, for example (see Chapter I of his *LA*), and it is already implicit in Wittgenstein's remark (*PI*, #73):

When someone defines the names of colours for me by pointing to samples and saying "This colour is called 'blue', this 'green'..." this case can be compared in many respects to putting a table in my hands, with the words written under the colour-samples. – Though this comparison may mislead in many ways. – One is now inclined to extend the comparison: to have understood the definition means to have in one's mind an idea of the thing defined, and that is a sample or picture. So if I am shewn various different leaves and told "This is called a 'leaf'", I get an idea of the shape of a leaf, a picture of it in my mind. – But what does the picture of a leaf look like when it does not shew us any particular shape, but 'what is common to all shapes of leaf'? Which shade is the 'sample in my mind' of the colour green – the sample which is common to all shades of green?

"But might there not be such 'general' samples? Say a schematic leaf, or a sample of *pure* green?" – Certainly there might. But for such a schema to be understood as a *schema*, and not as the shape of a particular leaf, and for a slip of pure green to be understood as a sample of all that is greenish and not as a sample of pure green – this in turn resides in the way the samples are used...

Whether something represents depends, in some sense, upon what people do with it. Resemblance may facilitate the acquisition of certain techniques for doing things, but it is the doings, and not their facilitation, which underly the representational function.

I shall have more to say about resemblance momentarily. What I want here to carry away from the painting of balloons is a certain ontological observation. What both indicates a balloon and portrays it as, say, red is a *single object* – a red, Q-shaped pigment patch. By virtue of being Q-shaped *it* (the patch) indicates a balloon, and by virtue of being red *it* (the patch) portrays as red the balloon which it indicates. The patch is not a *bare* particular, but it *is* a particular (an object) – it is a red, Q-shaped particular. Nor should it be confused with *the fact that* the patch is red and Q-shaped. The fact is assertible; the patch is not assertible. The object may be passed from hand to hand; the fact cannot be passed from hand to hand. What is true is that there would not *be* such an object as a red Q-shaped patch unless it *were* a fact that some patch is red and Q-shaped. But that should not lead one to confuse the two. What does the representing here is the object, not the fact. The object is *both* indicator *and* portrayal. In this case, it indicates by virtue of one of its features, portrays by virtue of another.

This point I wish to generalize. One of our political cartoons, for example, is both indicator and portrayal. *It* (the cartoon) indicates Nixon and *it* (the cartoon) portrays him as being of such-and-such a kind or character. So we have what might be called a "two-category, one-category" semantics for these simple representations. It is two-category in that each pigment patch both *indicates* a balloon and *portrays* it as being of such-and-such a color. It is one-category, however, because the indicator *is* the portrayal. It is not, of course, a portrayal in virtue of the same feature by virtue of which it indicates. It portrays that which it indicates as being such-and-such by virtue of *its* having some further property, e.g., by virtue of its being red. In the case of iconic depiction, the portrayed feature and the portraying feature may coincide. But this coincidence concerns resemblance and not representation. No necessity attaches to it. Thus, for example, limited to ink and paper, I might depict red balloons by cross-hatching and blue balloons by shading. But the logic of the case is the same. Its general pattern is this:

An *object*, X, indicates another *object*, Y, and portrays it as being φ (*by being itself* φ').

When the indication is indefinite, we may add that the object X indicates *a* Y *by being itself* ψ. How a definite indicator indicates, of course, remains to be discussed. The object X is both indicator and portrayal. It is a portrayal by virtue of being φ'. It is a φ'X (e.g., a red Q-shaped-patch).[1]

Let me now see to what extent these considerations can be carried over to a more complicated case – the case of *maps*. Here we can find, to begin with, the same pattern of indication and portrayal which we discerned in the case of our cartoons and balloons. Dots, for example, indicate cities; lines indicate roads. A line, however, not only *indicates* a road but also *portrays* it as being, say, unpaved or two-laned or divided. How it thus portrays the various characteristics of the road indicated is, as before, by virtue of having itself a certain character, φ'. For example, a line may portray a road as being unpaved (φ) by being itself dotted (φ'); as two-laned (φ) by being itself black (φ'); and as divided (φ) by being itself red (φ'). Similarly, a dot may portray a city as being under 5,000 or over 100,000 in population. Once again, portrayal is by virtue of the indicator's having itself a certain character. Thus a dot may indicate a city and portray it as being under 5,000 in population by being itself 2 mm in diameter; as being over 100,000 in population by being itself 5 mm in diameter; and so on. Again it is a single object (ink mark or pigment patch) which is both indicator and portrayal. Again, too, indefinite indication occurs by virtue of the representing object having a certain character, ψ: some ink marks indicate cities by virtue of their being dots (i.e., small and round); others indicate roads by virtue of their being lines (i.e., long and thin).

In the case of maps, however, we have two significant complications with which we need to come to grips. The first of these is the representation of *relational* states of affairs; the second, *definite* indication. Let me first look into relations.

One dot, *a*, indicates a city, A; another, *b*, a city, B. The indicated cities A and B are spatially related to one another. Let us say, for definiteness, that A is to the west of B. This information, too, is reflected on the map. How does this come about? Well, the instructions to the map reader are straightforward enough: If dot *a* is to the left of dot *b*, then the city which *a* indicates is to the west of the city which *b* indicates. What needs to be clarified is the ontological status of representation and represented. What I want to do is to hew to the model of one *object* representing another *object.*[2] In this case, however, what we have is one *group* of objects— o_1, $o_2, \ldots, o_n$ — representing another *group* of objects — $o'_1, o'_2, \ldots, o'_n$ — although this relation, in turn, will depend upon each object in the first group representing some one object in the second.

It will simplify the exposition of these sections if I introduce here a dispensible fiction — the notion of a *complex object.* And so I shall say something, *very briefly*, about what I will take to be the logic of complex objects. The notion is a dispensible one, a mere expository device, in the precise sense that everything which I shall say making use of it — by speaking of properties of and relations among complex objects — I *could* also say, although perhaps more circuitously, without it — by speaking of the properties of and relations among those objects which, as I shall say, *compose* the complexes. From time to time, I shall insert a reminder to this effect.

The main notion I shall employ is that of a *pair-object.* A pair-object, ⟨x,y⟩, has two disjoint objects, x and y, as *proper parts.* To say that x and y are disjoint is to say that they do not *overlap*, i.e., that no part of x is a part of y, and conversely. The pair-object ⟨x,y⟩ is completely constituted by its parts, x and y, in a certain order. To say that ⟨x,y⟩ is completely constituted by x and y is again to speak the language of part and whole. It is to say that whatever is a part of ⟨x,y⟩ is a part of x or of y or both. But to speak of "a certain order" is to step outside of the part-whole framework. It is to lay down a further identity condition for pair-objects. The condition is precisely what one would expect:

$$(u)\,(v)\,(\langle u,v \rangle = \langle x,y \rangle . \equiv . u = x \ \& \ v = y).$$

It will prove useful to be able to talk about relations between the parts of a pair-object in a way which makes reference only to the pair. A naive abbreviatory convention will do the trick. I shall say that a pair-object ⟨x,y⟩ is *R-connected* (and write 'R#⟨x,y⟩') if and only if its constituents x and y are related, in that order, by R:

$$R\#\langle x,y \rangle \ =_{df} \ xRy.$$

Being R-connected is sensibly predicable of any object, but — if R is a dyadic relation — it is only *truly* predicable of pairs:

$$R\#z \equiv (\exists x)\,(\exists y)\,(z = \langle x,y \rangle \ \& \ xRy).$$

These remarks, of course, generalize in the obvious way to triple-objects, quadruple-objects, and so on, connected by triadic and quadratic relations and the like.

The model I propose for understanding representation of (dyadic) relational states of affairs is that both representation and represented are objects, specifically *pair-objects*. In the case of the two cities A and B indicated by the two dots *a* and *b*, the *represented* object is a pair composed of the cities A and B: ⟨A,B⟩. The *representing* object, on the other hand, is a pair composed of the dots *a* and *b*; it is ⟨*a,b*⟩. The pattern of representation can then be the *same* as it was in the non-relational cases:

> One *object*, ⟨*a,b*⟩, indicates another object, ⟨A,B⟩, and portrays it as being φ by being itself φ'.

What are φ and φ' here? What property does the pair ⟨A,B⟩ have which needs to be represented? Since A is west of B, the pair is *west-connected*: West#⟨A,B⟩. And what property does the pair ⟨*a,b*⟩ have in virtue of which it portrays ⟨A,B⟩ as being west-connected? Well, *a* is to the left of *b*, so the pair is *left-connected*. φ, then, is *west#*, and φ' is *left#*:

> ⟨*a,b*⟩ indicates ⟨A,B⟩ and portrays it as being west# by being itself left#.[3]

This account is a relative of, although it departs significantly from, the Tractarian picture-theory account of representation which I have elucidated and championed in a variety of essays (*NPT*, *WTLP*, *WSC*). On that account, it would not be the left# *object* ⟨*a,b*⟩ which does the relevant representing in my example but rather the *fact that a* is to the left of *b*. The model offered in the *Tractatus*, in other words, is a

Fact represents (pictures) fact

model. On the Tractarian account, indicators and portrayals (in my present terminology) belong to *different* ontological categories. Indicators are objects, but portrayals are facts. On the account which I am presently offering, however, indicator and portrayal are both *objects* (or groups of objects). They are, in fact, the *same* object, although the functions of indication and portrayal will depend upon different characteristics of any single object. It is still too early to detail what dictates a choice between these two models, but I can anticipate the argument here by stating its conclusion: On Wittgenstein's view, metalinguistic discourse is impossible. The argument for this conclusion must wait, of course, until I have applied both models to the case of language proper. It is sufficient here to highlight the two accounts and the locus of their difference. They differ in the *ontological* account which they give of the vehicle of representation. It may seem that this is an odd sort of thing to be considering in the first place. But it is not. As I hope to show, it is in an important sense the essence of the matter.

The extension of my account of relational map representation to relations of higher polyadicity is straightforward. Triadic relations yield complex triple-objects; quadratic relations, complex quadruple-objects; and so on. In all of these cases, we can hew to a *single* pattern of analysis:

> (Complex) object o_1, indicates (complex) object o_2 and portrays it as being φ by being itself φ'.

Before proceeding to consider language proper, however, there is a second complication which must be addressed in the case of maps. A specific dot does not simply (indefinitely) indicate *a city*. If the map is of any use at all, the dot must (definitely) indicate *some particular city*, say Boston or Philadelphia. What this remark suggests is that there are *two distinct sorts* of map-territory correlations which together contribute to representation. One sort we have been dealing with for some time. It is the correlations between map-marks of certain *kinds* or *characteristics* with territorial features of certain *kinds* or *characteristics* — thus, dots with cities, lines with roads, *large* dots with *populous* cities, *red* lines with *divided* roads, left# dot-pairs with west# city-pairs, and so on. For a map to represent a *particular* territory, however, we must supplement these *generic* correlations with *specific* correlations, between *individual* dots and *particular* cities, individual lines and particular roads. And it will be correlations of this second, specific, sort — however they come about — that form the extensional counterpart of definite indication.

This way of looking at things highlights the fact that what I have been calling "indefinite indication" is a sham. For indefinite indication is simply definite portrayal. But it is the portrayal of *kinds* rather than the portrayal of *characteristics*. 'Indication' and 'portrayal' were to mark a *functional* distinction in the semantics of representation. But there is no functional distinction between what I've been calling "indefinite indication" and what I've been calling "portrayal". Both consist in correlations of representing objects which have certain features with represented objects which have certain (typically different) features. Thus, for example, where I earlier put

> a Q-shaped pigment patch indicates a balloon and portrays it as being red by being itself red,

I might equally have put

> a red pigment patch indicates something red and portrays it as being a balloon by being itself Q-shaped[4]

or even

> a pigment patch indicates something and portrays it as being a red balloon by being itself both red and Q-shaped.

Analogously, in the case of maps I have said that dots indicate cities, but I might equally well have said that ink marks indicate geographical features and portray some of them as being cities by being themselves dots.

For definite indication, however, this trick will not work. Thus we cannot paraphrase

> a certain picture indicates George Washington and portrays him as a sallow-complexioned Viking prince

by

> a certain picture indicates *something* and portrays it as *being George Washington* and...

for it is not clear how we are to continue. What we would need is presumably something like

> ... portrays it *as* being George Washington (portrayed?) *as* a sallow-complexioned Viking prince,

but this *nesting* of portrayals is not what is portrayed by the picture as originally described. Besides, indicating *something* and portraying it *as* being George Washington is *not* the same as indicating George Washington. A political cartoonist, for example, thinking of Richard Nixon as founding a new American order, might draw a cartoon of Richard Nixon as George Washington, i.e., a cartoon which indicates Richard Nixon and portrays him as being George Washington. But it would not be a cartoon *of* George Washington (i.e., a cartoon which *indicates* George Washington). To portray Richard Nixon as George Washington is to portray Nixon as possessing certain salient *characteristics* of George Washington; it is not to represent Nixon as identical to (one and the same person as) George Washington.

Perhaps, then, one will be tempted to introduce the characteristic of *being identical to George Washington* — a characteristic uniquely possessed by George Washington — and to parse the original picture by saying that it

> indicates *something* and portrays it as *being identical to* George Washington and as being a sallow-complexioned Viking prince.

This should remind us of Quine's "reduction" of proper names to such predicates as 'Socratizes' and 'Pegasizes' (*OWTI*; *W&O*, 176ff.). But there are several considerations which militate against this gambit. Most obviously, it is a fraud. For when we ask, as one is likely to do with quantifiers, what *is* the *something* indicated by our picture and portrayed as being identical to George Washington, the answer must surely be that it is *George Washington*; and, if that is the case, why not say so? The point here is that, as Kripke has persuasively argued (*I&N*, *NN*), anything possessing the putative property of being identical to George Washington is *necessarily* identical to George Washington. Only George Washington *could* possess that putative property. And that being the case, it is chimerical to speak of a *property* here at all. For a property is — one would like to say *essentially* is — something which any of a plurality of particulars could exemplify.[5]

I suspect, in fact, that the proposed reduction of proper names to identity-predications makes sense only against a background which has already been discredited. This is the supposition, examined and rejected in Chapter II, that a name names what it does because it is associated with a *cluster* of properties jointly exemplified uniquely by the named object. For only this supposition lends the least credibility to the view that the indicating of *specific, particular* individuals in the world could be channeled entirely through predicates and quantification. Only if one supposes that proper names attain reference through having associated with them an ambient, perhaps open-textured, set of predicates the applicability of which to an object is *criterial* for that object's being the referent of the name is one likely to believe that one might as well precipitate these ambient criteria out *directly* into a uniquely ascribable identity predicate. But if this is not so, the name 'George Washington' will occur *essentially* in the putative predicate 'is identical to George Washington' which becomes, then, a predicate by syntactic courtesy only. Appeal to predicates of *this* sort, however, makes no logical advance on the semantic problems of definite indication.

I shall take it, then, that we have two irreducible sets of correlations between map and territory. One, corresponding to (definite) indication, is a matching up of individual map-marks with particular geographical structures. The other, corresponding to portrayal (now including indefinite indication), is a matching up of map-marks having certain *features* (of certain kinds or characteristics) with geographical structures having certain features.

We must still ask, however, in what these "correlations" *consist, how*, for example, particular map-marks of certain kinds and characteristics come to be "matched up with" particular geographical structures of certain kinds and characteristics. And the answer to *that* question brings us squarely to language proper. For, I shall argue, indication and portrayal — in the case of

maps and in the case of iconic pictures – are *logically parasitic* upon   designation and claiming in language.

The point is not simply that the dots and lines on actual maps are *labeled*,
so that the designator 'Boston', for example, occurs together with the dot
which indicates Boston. That, of course, is true, but the point goes deeper
than that. For consider how one could come to use a map *none* of the dots
or lines of which are labeled. What one would have to do is to *fit* the map to
some territory. Now how would we proceed?

Here is one procedure: *Suppose* that the map represents some (familiar)
territory. Suppose, in particular, that we already know that the dots indicate (indefinitely) *cities* and the lines *roads*. There is no necessity about
this, of course, but let us, for convenience, posit a rich set of prior information of this sort, since it alters nothing in principle. We can look at the complications in a moment. Thus suppose even that we know that *large* dots
represent cities of large population, *red* lines represent divided roads, left#
dot-pairs represent west# city-pairs, and so on. Suppose, in other words,
that we are provided with a complete *key*. This information in hand, we
label the dots (1, 2, 3, . . .) and the lines (*a, b, c,* . . .) and, using the key,
produce a list of *truths* about the territory – whatever it is – which the map
represents:

> 1 is a city over 100,000 in population
> City 2 is west of City 1
> City 1 is joined to City 2 by a divided road, *a*
> .
> .
> .

To interpret the map, then, what we need is a *translation scheme.* In
essence, we produce an hypothesis: City 1 is New York, City 2 is Pittsburgh,
Road *a* is the Pennsylvania Turnpike,... which correlates *map-indicators* with
designators. We have fitted the map to the territory, then, when our translation hypothesis takes indefinite map-territory truths into definite truths
about some known territory:

> New York is a city over 100,000 in population
> Pittsburgh is west of New York
> New York is joined to Pittsburgh by the (divided) Pennsylvania
> Turnpike
> .
> .
> .

I have, of course, provided the potential map-user with a great deal of information in the form of a fully articulated *key*. If one comes to the problem of interpretation with innocent eye and innocent mind, however, he is not that fortunate. Dots may indefinitely indicate trees and lines irrigation ditches or, for that matter, the whole inked pattern may be an inelegant attempt at ornamental design. Yet the epistemology of this informationally impoverished situation is formally no different. The problem faced is still one of translation, although now we face a *multiple* translation task. The process can be represented as consisting of several *steps*. The first of these is a *description of the map-marks in an (extensional) map vocabulary:*

> The map consists of *dots* of various *sizes* in various *relations* to one another on the page connected by *lines* of various *colors*.

Now, labeling the map-marks quite arbitrarily, we arrive at a set of *truths about the map:*

1 is a dot	1 is 5 mm in diameter
2 is a dot	2 is 5 mm in diameter
•	•
•	•
•	•
a is a line	*a* is red
•	*b* is black
•	•
•	•

⟨1,2⟩ is left# (i.e., 1 is left of 2)
⟨1,4⟩ is above# (i.e., 1 is above 4)
    •
    •
    •

The next step gives us a key. We advance the *hypotheses*:

'dot'	⟷	'city'
'line'	⟷	'road'
'left#'	⟷	'west#'
•		
•		
•		

These translational hypotheses correspond to the *generic* correlations of map and territory. A second set of hypotheses yields the *specific* correlations:

'1'	$\longleftrightarrow$	'New York'
'2'	$\longleftrightarrow$	'Pittsburgh'
'a'	$\longleftrightarrow$	'the Pennsylvania Turnpike'

.
.
.

In terms of these hypotheses, we may *translate* the true claims about the map (framed in the extensional map vocabulary) into *claims about a territory:*

New York is a city   New York is over 100,000 in
                                  population

Pittsburgh is a city
.   .

.   .

.   US 7 is a two-lane highway

Interstate 50 is a road   .

.   .

.   .

Pittsburgh is west of New York
Albany is north of New York
.

.

.

If the translation takes the true claims about the map into *true* claims about a known territory, the map *fits* that territory. We conclude, then, that the map is a map *of* that territory, and, by deploying the translation schemes thus evolved, we may use it to find our way about. Interpreting a map is thus *essentially* language-mediated. It requires a (linguistic) *description* of the map and a *translation* of that description from an extensional map vocabulary into the geographical vocabulary descriptive of the territory mapped.

The argument here, it must now be remarked, is perfectly general. And this comes as somewhat of a surprise. But let me survey the case for iconic depiction. There are two main views of how it comes about that a picture depicting, say, George Washington as a sallow-compexioned Viking prince indicates George Washington and portrays him as sallow-complexioned and as a Viking prince. The one is the resemblance theory; the other, intentionalistic. What we are now in a position to see is that these two views in the end come to the same thing — and that what they come to is translation. I have already remarked on the way in which resemblance cannot, *per se*, be constitutive of representation. And I have also remarked on what resemblance in fact amounts to in several sample cases. What I wish to propose now, however, is that the process of limning the relations of resemblance putatively obtaining between picture and represented object precisely is the process of providing something strictly analogous to a *key* for map-interpretation. On the resemblance theory, the process of interpreting a picture is the process of noting resemblances between features of the picture and objects in the world. The picture is then supposed to represent, on the pure form of the theory, that which it maximally resembles. This latter cannot, of course, be the case, for a variety of reasons adverted to earlier (See, again, Goodman, *LA*, Chapter 1). More importantly, however, what in fact get counted as *representationally relevant* resemblances between picture and world cannot be simply *noted*. Rather, one learns to interpret pictures as one learns to interpret maps. One learns that certain picture-features indefinitely indicate objects of a certain kind or portray them as having certain characteristics. Resemblance *per se* is not here to the point. It concerns, paradigmatically, the consilience of the representing characteristic (thus, the red color of a Q-shaped pigment patch) and the characteristic portrayed (thus, the red color of the indicated balloon). Derivatively, it concerns the specifiability of a relatively compact physical relationship (e.g., two-dimensional orthogonal projection) between the representing characteristic and the kind or characteristic indicated or portrayed. And ultimately, and still more derivatively, resemblance concerns the *ease* or *naturalness* with which a set of translation rules are learned for a given mode of depiction (thus, color photographs are "more realistic" than portraits in oils).

Epistemologically, however, the process of interpreting a picture in the absence of prior knowledge concerning pictorial conventions is multiple translation. To recur to our crude balloon paintings, at the first level we have true descriptions of the canvas in an extensional picture vocabulary:

> 1 is a Q-shaped pigment patch
> 2 is a Q-shaped pigment patch

> .
> .
> .

        1 is red
        2 is blue
            •

            •

            •

and, at the second level, translations of these into derived descriptions of a
represented subject-matter by means of a key:

    'is a Q-shaped pigment patch'   ⟷   'is a balloon'
    'is red'   ⟷   'is red'
    'is blue'   ⟷   'is blue'
            •

            •

            •

Here is where *resemblance* comes in: The more "realistic" the depiction, the
more we can utilize the *homophonic* translation hypothesis in the construction of the key.

    If indication is indefinite, this is the end of the process.

        1 is a red balloon
        2 is a blue balloon
            •

            •

            •

We conclude that our picture is *of* variously colored balloons. If indication
is definite, however, we can take the third step by proposing such translation hypotheses as:

    '1'   ⟷   'the object in Tom's hand'
    '2'   ⟷   'the object in Dick's hand'
            •

            •

            •

to arrive at a set of claims about a subject-matter framed in a vocabulary
appropriate for describing it:

        The object in Tom's hand is a red balloon
        The object in Dick's hand is a blue balloon
            •

            •

            •

And if these claims are *true* claims about a particular known subject-matter, we may conclude that the picture represents that subject-matter.

The preservable core of the resemblance theory is thus the same translation into linguistic representations which formed the core of map-representation. And the same is true of the intentionalistic theory. On this view, the subject-matter of a depiction is a function of the artist's *intentions*. A picture is *of*, say, George Washington (indicates him) by virtue of the artist's intention to paint George Washington. Now I have already argued that what constitutes the artist's intention to paint George Washington rather than, say, Abraham Lincoln, must be viewed on the model of securing reference to George Washington rather than to Abraham Lincoln. And this, in turn, requires us to posit something which is functionally a *designator* of George Washington, though structurally covert, conceived on analogy with overt designators of George Washington (i.e., with the name 'George Washington'). Representation in intention or thought can no more be *constituted* by relations of resemblance than can representation in watercolor pictures. (See Dennett, *C&C*, 132–46.) Thus the intentionalistic theory, too, cashes out iconic depiction in terms of linguistic representation, although at the higher level of generality in which both overt speech and covert thought are systems of linguistic representation.

Let me pause here to collect a few morals. If what I have been saying is correct, linguistic representation is *the* basic, non-derivative mode of representation. Iconic representation, representation by maps, and so on represent the world only derivatively, by being *translatable* into the linguistic mode. Interpreting a picture or reading a map, I have argued, is a task epistemologically on a par with translating a language. Thus the logic of linguistic representation is not *explained* by likening it to the logic of iconic depiction or some other *non-linguistic* mode of representation. What consideration of non-linguistic systems of representation does do for us, however, is highlight the *ontology* of the vehicles of representation and focus our attention on two sets of *correlations* between representing objects and represented objects. The ontology is an ontology of *objects*, simple and complex, and the correlations *specific* and *generic* – the specific matching individual representing objects with individual represented objects; the generic matching representing objects of certain kinds or having certain characteristics with represented objects of certain (typically different) kinds or having certain (typically different) characteristics. And with this in hand, I am at last prepared to turn to language.

By a *basic claim*, I mean, roughly, a simple indicative declarative sentence – a sentence which is not truth-functionally or quantificationally complex, which contains neither subordinate clauses (e.g., that-clauses) nor what I have called "terms of semantic appraisal" ('couldn't', 'must', etc.) — in which *all the designators are proper names.*

Basic claims are the natural language counterparts of the *atomic propositions* of logical calculus. That there *are*, in this sense, basic claims, I take to be completely uncontroversial. Examples can be multiplied indefinitely: 'Maxine is hungry', 'Albany is east of Buffalo', 'Hermann introduced Eva to Adolph', and so on.

I should like to reintroduce here the convenient fiction of the Author — which I sketched and defended in Chapter III — subject, for present purposes, to a further limitation. The Author, recall, was a being — otherwise quite like us — whose covert thoughts are matched one-for-one with overt inscribed claims. The limitation which I wish temporarily to impose is this: that the Author inscribes all and only those *basic* claims warranted by his entries to and inferential moves within the network of claim-positions constituted by his espoused system of content rules. The public product of his epistemological activities, then, will be a rich set of basic claims — basic, since he inscribes only those, and rich, since he inscribes *all* which his espoused linguistic normatives warrant. I shall call this the "Basic World Story".

I have already distinguished in language the functions of designation and claiming. These I mapped onto the generic notions of representation of objects and representation of states of affairs. For non-linguistic representation I had an analogous pair of mappings onto the generic notions: indication and portrayal. But here the parallelism would seem to break down, for while we find for non-linguistic representation the unpacking:

$$x \text{ indicates } a \text{ and portrays it as being } \varphi$$

for linguistic representation, we have simply:

$$x \text{ claims that } a \text{ is } \varphi$$

where 'x' in each of these cases stands proxy for an expression which designates a vehicle of representation (picture, map-mark, sentence, etc.). What I wish first to suggest is that the breakdown in parallelism is merely apparent. In other words, I want to construe the ontology of the vehicles of *linguistic* representation on the model of the ontology of the vehicles of *non-linguistic* representation.

To this end, I propose that we transmute

$$x \text{ claims that } a \text{ is } \varphi$$

through the forms

> x claims *a* to be φ

and

> x claims of *a* that it is φ

to the canonical pattern:

> x *designates a* and *claims of it* that it is φ.

This is an artificial and strained mode of speech, to be sure, but it highlights what needs highlighting. For just as we could work with the scheme

> x indicates *a* and portrays it as (being) φ

to argue that portrayals *are* indicators, so we may use the scheme

> x designates *a* and claims of it that it is φ

to argue that claims *are* designators.

   For the protosemantics of claiming, I wish to suggest, are the *same* as the protosemantics of portrayal. In the case of portrayal, we had, as a general case,

> x indicates y and portrays it as being φ *by being itself* φ'.

I propose to complete the scheme for claiming in the same way:

> x designates *a* and claims of it that it is φ *by being itself* φ'.

In our balloon pictures, φ' stood proxy for such empirical characteristics of Q-shaped pigment patches as being red or being crosshatched. What I am here proposing is that φ' in the scheme for *claiming* stands proxy for various *empirical characteristics of proper-name inscriptions*. What might these empirical characteristics be?

   Consider the sample sentence-inscription

> (1)   Eunice is pink.

As I am parsing the protosemantics of (1), I want to say of it that

> (1) designates Eunice and claims of her that she is pink.

In order to do this, however, I must adopt a certain view of the *ontology* of (1).

   Traditionally, (1) is parsed as a *complex* object. Specifically, (in my terminology, and assimilating the copula to the predicate) (1) is standardly treated as the *pair-object* ⟨'Eunice', 'is pink'⟩, the disjoint parts of which are connected by the relation of (dyadic) concatenation (in my notation: ⟨'Eunice', 'is pink'⟩ is concat2#). And I shall make *use* of this traditional (subject-predicate) parsing in speaking of the 'Eunice' part of (1) and of the 'is pink' part of (1). But the *whole burden* of my current discussion is to provide an alternative ontological construal of (1) which will serve as a fundamentum of the analysis of how (1) represents.

Thus, in line with my previous discussions, in order to say of (1) that it designates Eunice and claims of her that she is pink, I must construe (1) as *the proper-name inscription 'Eunice'*, itself having a certain characteristic. To do this, I shall treat what is *traditionally* the 'is pink' part of inscription (1) as doing a radically different job from what is traditionally the 'Eunice' part of (1). The 'is pink' part will have to enter into the *ascription of an empirical characteristic* to the 'Eunice' part. But what empirical characteristics does the 'Eunice' part of (1) have?

Well, there are many. It is, for example, about 1/2 inch long. It is also black. Neither of these empirical features, however, engages the 'is pink' part of (1). It is not too difficult, though, to locate an empirical characteristic of the 'Eunice' part which does. The 'Eunice' part has this empirical feature: It has an 'is pink' to its right. Now *having an 'is pink' to the right* may not seem on the face of it to be a candidate empirical characteristic of proper-name inscriptions, but it undeniably *is* an empirical property of *some* proper-name inscriptions. For example, it is a property of the inscriptions of 'Maybelle' and of 'Jerome' in

(2)   Maybelle is pink

and

(3)   Jerome is pink,

as well as of the inscription of 'Eunice' in (1). It will prove helpful to have an abbreviated notation for ascribing this feature to proper-name inscriptions. Let me use 'R-pink*' for this purpose. Thus, for example, I shall say that, in (1), the 'Eunice' is R-pink*; in (2), the 'Maybelle' is R-pink*; and so on.

In fact, the protosemantic ontological parsing I wish to assign to (1) holds that (1) *is an R-pink* 'Eunice'.* (2), similarly, is an R-pink* 'Maybelle' and (3) an R-pink* 'Jerome'. To say that (1) *is* an R-pink* 'Eunice' is exactly parallel to saying that one of our balloon pictures is a red Q-shaped pigment patch. And just as a red Q-shaped pigment patch is a Q-shaped pigment patch, so an R-pink* 'Eunice' *is* a 'Eunice'. The *claim* (1) thus *is* the *designator* 'Eunice'.

To recapitulate, the ontological parsing of the inscription (1) is not unique. A traditional and standard way of parsing (1) sees it as a complex pair-object, ⟨'Eunice', 'is pink'⟩, composed of two disjoint simple parts, 'Eunice' and 'is pink', related by being concatenated the one with the other. My protosemantic ontological parsing of the inscription (1), however, sees it as a *single simple* object, a 'Eunice' inscription, having a (complex) property: it is an *R-pink** 'Eunice' inscription.

This point of view extends in the natural way to relational claims. Consider, for example,

(4)   Maude despises Elmo.

The classical account of the ontology of inscription (4) parses it as what I have earlier called a *triple-object:*

⟨'Maude', 'despises', 'Elmo'⟩

composed of three simple parts related by (triadic) concatenation.[6] On the protosemantic view, however, I again attempt to attain a parsing in which inscription (4) is a single (now *complex*) designator having a certain empirical characteristic. The designator in question will be a designator of the pair-object ⟨Maude, Elmo⟩ and will *itself* be a pair-object, composed of the designators, 'Maude' and 'Elmo', of the constituents, Maude and Elmo, of the original pair. Thus inscription (4) will be viewed as the pair-object ⟨'Maude', 'Elmo'⟩, and the empirical characteristic in virtue of which (4) claims of Maude and Elmo that the former despises the latter will be the property of being R-connected (R#) for some dyadic relation R. What relation R will do the job?

Well, what *are* the empirical relations between the designators 'Maude' and 'Elmo' in the inscription (4)? Again, there are many. 'Maude' is longer than 'Elmo', for example; and 'Elmo' is to the right of 'Maude'. Neither of these relations, however, engages what, on the traditional reading, is the 'despises' part of (4). It is again not difficult, though, to find an empirical relation between 'Maude' and 'Elmo' which does. 'Maude' and 'Elmo' *stand respectively to the left and right of a 'despises'*. Let me call *this* complex empirical relation 'LR-despises*'. The pair-object ⟨'Maude', 'Elmo'⟩ then has the corresponding empirical *characteristic* of being LR-despises*-*connected* (LR-despises*#).

Being despises# is an empirical characteristic of pair-objects in the world which are composed of two persons the first of whom despises the second. *Being LR-despises*#* is an empirical characteristic of pair-objects in the world, as well. But, like being R-pink*, the objects of which *it* is a characteristic answer *also* to pure normative characterizations. They are natural *linguistic* objects; specifically, *designator-pairs* — pair-objects composed of two designators, the first of which, in this case, stands to the left of a 'despises' which stands to the left of the second.

I shall thus conclude that inscription (4) *is* the LR-despises*# designator-pair ⟨'Maude', 'Elmo'⟩ and write

⟨'Maude', 'Elmo'⟩ designates ⟨Maude, Elmo⟩ and claims it to be despises# by being itself LR-despises*#.

The general pattern of protosemantic analysis, then, extends in this way to dyadic relational basic claims and, analogously, to triadic, quadratic, pentadic, etc. relational basic claims as well.

I arrive, then, at an ontological parsing of our representing system — the Basic World Story inscribed by the Author — which views it as consisting of objects *all* of which are designator-inscriptions. Like the objects represented, these representing objects are of various kinds (e.g., some of them are 'Maude's, some 'Elmo's, etc.), have various characteristics (some of them are R-pink*, some R-yellow*, some R-tall*, etc.), and stand in various relations to one another (one may be LR-despises* another, one LR-taller* another, one LR-west-of* another, and so on). If this system of natural linguistic objects represents another system of objects in the world, then, I propose that there will be, as in the case of maps, two sets of *protocorrelations* between the two systems — one specific and one generic.

The *specific* protocorrelations match up designator-inscriptions (representing objects) with represented objects (and designator-pairs with represented pair-objects, etc.)

The *generic* protocorrelations match up designator-inscriptions having certain characteristics φ'_1, φ'_2, ... with represented objects having certain (different) characteristics φ_1, φ_2, ... (and LR-X*# designator-pairs with X# represented pair-objects, etc.)

For example, 'Maude' will match up with Maude, 'Elmo' with Elmo, R-pink* designators with pink objects, R-tall* designators with tall objects, LR-despises*# designator-pairs with despises# pair-objects, and so on. By "match up" here, I mean precisely that the two systems of objects will be (*ideally*) *extensionally isomorphic* to one another, in particular, that *regularities of co-occurrence and exclusion* among the empirical characteristics of the represented objects will be mirrored by corresponding regularities of co-occurrence and exclusion among the empirical characteristics of the representing objects in virtue of which the latter are the claims which they are. And, if this is correct, the solution to the original problem of representation can now be stated.

The original problem, recall, was the question of how it is that language represents a non-linguistic world. The answer which I propose is that the one represents the other by being *structurally* a system of objects in the natural order (natural linguistic objects) *protocorrelated* with the system of non-linguistic objects represented and (ideally) extensionally isomorphic to that system of non-linguistic objects. Specifically, for example, we will have

> 'Eunice is pink' designates Eunice and claims of her that she is pink by being an R-pink* 'Eunice', since 'Eunice' is protocorrelated with Eunice and R-pink* designators with pink objects,

and we will have

> 'Maude despises Elmo' designates ⟨Maude, Elmo⟩ and claims of it that it is despises# (if you prefer: designates Maude and Elmo and claims of them that the former despises the latter) by being an LR-despises*# ⟨'Maude', 'Elmo'⟩, since ⟨'Maude', 'Elmo'⟩ is protocorrelated with ⟨Maude, Elmo⟩ (derivatively, since 'Maude' is protocorrelated with Maude and 'Elmo' with Elmo) and LR-despises*# designator-pairs with despises# pair-objects (if you prefer: and pairs of designators which are LR-despises* to one another with pairs of objects such that the one despises the other).

Now this may appear terribly uninformative. Worse yet, it may appear *false*, for, it may be asked, what guarantees that the system of natural linguistic objects (designator-inscriptions) variously characterized and related *is* thus (even ideally) extensionally isomorphic to the system of natural non-linguistic objects represented? Why should we suppose that these protocorrelations between the Basic World Story, viewed structurally in extension, and the world exist at all? It is precisely to answer *this* question that I have engaged in the extensive epistemological investigations of the earlier chapters.

The key point is that the variously characterized and related designator-inscriptions which are structurally protocorrelated with the represented world are *also*, functionally, *normative* linguistic objects. That is, *they are produced by a representer according to rules.*

The rules in question, I have argued, are the *content rules* of the language, systematically constitutive of positions as claims in the game-language analogy. What from the intentional point of view are linguistic normatives, however, are, from the extensional point of view, constraints on the tokening behavior of language users. Sellars phrases the point nicely (*T&C*, 216): "Espousal of principles is reflected in uniformities of performance." What are, intentionally, normative constraints on conceptual activity are necessarily reflected in the system of inscriptions (overt or covert) which is the extensional product in the natural order of that conceptual activity.

Now this still would carry us no distance if the content rules of a language were free creations of the language users – that is, if what rules are espoused were a matter for arbitrary decision. But I have argued that the content rules of a language are the *material* rules of a language-*qua*-theory. Empirical inquiry is the process of coming to espouse rules of inference constitutive of the concepts they govern. And inquiry is not an arbitrary process. It has constraints. Specifically, inquiry is *causally* informed by the action of the empirical world upon the representers in it. Empirical inquiry, I argued, is essentially inference to an explanation. And explanation, in turn, was identified with the redescription of phenomena to give them places in a unified and coherent conceptual framework constituted by a system of material rules of inference – the same rules which are the *content* rules of the theoretical language. But whether a specific conceptual scheme, thus construed, is explanatorily adequate to a particular range of empirical phenomena is not a matter for arbitrary decision. The explanatory adequacy of a conceptual system depends, rather, upon the continuing experiences of the community of inquirers. It is because a language is the *evolutionary product* of the continuing *causal* impact of anomalous experiential inputs to the community of representers that the structure of its *extensional* realization tends increasingly towards protocorrelational isomorphism with the world represented.

Finally, the content rules of a language were identified with the rules of *truth* for claims framed in that language. Empirical truth was identified as assertibility in accordance with the material rules of an adequate explanatory theory, making use of whatever collateral considerations the rules themselves impose. In doing so, I came to view the Principle of Charity as the methodological fallout of a necessary truth – that the majority of empirical claims of a population of language users must be (synchronically speaking) true. We thus found common ground for the traditionally competing pragmatic and coherence theories of truth. For, while empirical truth is, as the pragmatists would hold, a variety of warranted assertibility, *what* warrants the assertibility of claims are the material rules of a theory accepted on the grounds of its explanatory power. And that, in turn, is its ability to offer redescriptions of phenomena assimilating them to an increasingly *integrated and coherent* conceptual framework.

I am now in a position to weld the classical *correspondence* theory of truth to this structure. For we have seen that what is *intentionally* an increasingly coherent conceptual framework generates *extensionally*, by virtue of its being the causal evolutionary product of the action of the world upon the community of representers, a system of natural linguistic objects within that world and protocorrelated with it. And this is just to say that, in the limit, there *will be* a correspondence between language and the world precisely in the sense that individual designators may be mapped onto individual objects, and, speaking loosely, *kinds* of designators onto *kinds* of objects (e.g., R-pink* designators onto pink objects, etc.) in such a way that the resulting structures are *extensionally isomorphic* to each other. Since language represents the non-linguistic world precisely by being protocorrelated with it, we can now assert that correspondence, in this sense, rather than being constitutive of *truth*, is a precondition of the *possibility of representation in general.* Yet correspondence forms the substance of matter-of-factual truth as well. For, since the content rules of a language *are* the rules of truth for that language, the majority of empirical claims of a population of language users must be (synchronically speaking) true – and to say that they must be true comes to the same thing as to say that they must facilitate the protocorrelations by virtue of which they come to represent the world at all. I think that this is the *deep* truth underlying Wittgenstein's remark (*PI*, #242):

If language is to be a means of communication there must be agreement not only in definitions but also (queer as this may sound) in judgments. This seems to abolish logic, but does not do so. – It is one thing to describe methods of measurement, and another to obtain and state results of measurement. But what we call "measuring" is partly determined by a certain constancy in results of measurement.

My quarrel with this passage is largely that it is not sufficiently "queer". For, if what I have been arguing is correct, "agreement in judgments" is not a precondition of communication merely but of the possibility of representative language *überhaupt.*

Yet in saying that correspondence, *qua* protocorrelation, forms the substance of matter-of-factual truth, we must not make the mistake of interpreting this claim as the claim that correspondence is the *criterion* of truth. To do so is to fall once again into the error of supposing a concept-free yet cognitive epistemological commerce with the world ("The Myth of the

Given"). Just as I argued earlier that the possession of empirical truth is the necessary *outcome* of explanatory theorizing but cannot be the end-in-view *controlling* the theoretical enterprise, so, here, correspondence as proto-correlational isomorphism is the *outcome* of the evolution of representational systems, but cannot be the *grounds* upon which a choice among representational systems is predicated, for that our system of representations is, in extension, protocorrelated with the world it represents can be known to be the case only, as it were, *indirectly* – through our knowing that the system of linguistic normatives giving rise to the system of natural linguistic objects protocorrelated with the world which they thereby represent is increasingly explanatorily adequate to that world as it impinges upon us through continuing experience.

The traditional correspondence, coherence, and pragmatic theories of *truth* can thus be seen as locating three dimensions of the process of *representation*. The pragmatic theory locates the *epistemological* fundamentum: the production of natural linguistic objects (variously qualified designator-inscriptions) under the control of content rules which are material rules of inference for the language-*qua*-theory and the rules of truth for claims framed in terms of the concepts which they constitute. The correspondence theory locates the *ontological* fundamentum: the *extensional* protocorrelations between the system of representing objects and the system of represented objects in virtue of which the one represents the other. And the coherence theory locates the *methodological* fundamentum: the end-in-view of evolving increasingly coherent and integrated conceptual structures to which anomalous experiential data can be assimilated and, thereby, explained.

Now it cannot be too quickly stressed that this account is a radical simplification of the current actual situation. It is the *limit* account, as the Basic World Story is a *limiting* story, and so the extensional isomorphism of protocorrelation between language and the world is, in its way, as much a regulative ideal as the Peircean limit to which actual physical theories tend. In the next chapter, I shall try to make good *some* of the simplifications with which I have been operating. Specifically, I shall have to discuss, first, *complex* claims, including truth-functional compounds of basic claims and quantificational claims, and, second, the *availability of designators* and basic claims in physical theories which, I have argued, are the model for empirical descriptive (matter-of-factual) language in general. In that way, I can begin to bring the *idealized* picture of representation which I have been developing back to the realities in which we live and move – to our current shared form of life.

Before doing so, however, there is one topic earlier left in abeyance which I must discuss, one promissory note to be cashed in this chapter. I earlier contrasted my present account of the protosemantics of representation with the fact-pictures-fact model offered in the *Tractatus*. And I suggested then that what dictates the assimilation of *both* indicators *and* portrayals (both designators and claims) to the category of (natural linguistic) *objects* – in contrast to Wittgenstein's Tractarian assimilation of designators to objects and claims to *facts* – is that a metalanguage is impossible on the Tractarian view. I am now in a position to complete that argument.

On the Tractarian account, the claim

(1)   Sissypuss is furry

is to be construed as a *fact*, the fact (in my terminology) that 'Sissypuss' is R-furry*. Now the minimal sort of claim which we should like to be able to make in a metalanguage is

(2)   'Sissypuss' occurs in 'Sissypuss is furry'.

On my current view, (2) is straightforward. I parse (1) as an R-furry* 'Sissypuss' – an *object* – and the sense of (2) is captured by

(3)   'Sissypuss' is a *part* of 'Sissypuss is furry'

(here, on my view, not of course a *proper* part). The ' 'Sissypuss is furry' ' in (2) is simply *another* natural linguistic object designating that object, the R-furry* 'Sissypuss', which, on my view, the claim (1) *is*.

On the Tractarian view, however, (1) is not an object but a fact. What, then, are we to make of the ' 'Sissypuss is furry' ' in (2)? Well, *it* must be an object, for (2) is a claim of the form 'xRy' and, on Wittgenstein's account, any claim of that form is a fact, the fact that 'x' and 'y' stand in a certain relation. The parsing of (2), then, must be that (2) is the fact that ' 'Sissypuss' ' and ' 'Sissypuss is furry' ' are LR-occurs-in*, and its sense must be given by something like

(4)   ' 'Sissypuss' ' is a constituent of the fact that 'Sissypuss' is R-furry*,

for (1) is supposed to *be* the fact that 'Sissypuss' is R-furry* and the ' 'Sissypuss is furry' ' in (2) is supposed to designate that fact which (1) is.

These considerations imply that Wittgenstein must view quotation marks as a device for forming *designators* of *facts*. The quotation marks in ' 'Sissypuss is furry' ' in (2), in other words, do putatively the job of 'the fact that...' in (4). But *can* any linguistic device do that job?

Let us carve up (2) in the following way for discussion:

'$\underline{Sissypuss}$' occurs in '$\underline{Sissypuss\ is\ furry}$'

|_____ α _____| δ |_____ β _____| γ

In order to understand (2) as a truth, on the Tractarian view, I am suggesting that we must see it this way: recognize α in β, recognize β as a linguistic *fact*, and recognize γ as a *designator*. Can we do this? For γ to be a designator, it must be a linguistic *object* standing in RL-occurs-in* to δ. For (2) to say what it's supposed to say, β must be a *fact*, the fact which γ putatively designates. Yet β is supposed to be a *part* of γ. And this is ontologically incoherent.

One can't state *parts* of objects any more than one can state objects (on pain of making nonsense of 'part'). Yet β is supposed to be a fact – the fact (1), that 'Sissypuss' is R-furry* – so I can state it, *and* a part of γ – which must be a linguistic *object* in order for me to be able to state (2). But nothing intelligible can be made of the putative *relation* between the linguistic *fact* which β has to be and the linguistic *object* which γ has to be.

Wittgenstein claims in the *Tractatus* that some things can only be *shown*, and that what can be shown *cannot* be said. We have now uncovered the roots of that contention. The reason one cannot say what can be shown is that Wittgenstein's protosemantics of representation allows no consistent *ontological* parsing of a sentence which *purports* to say what is shown. On Wittgenstein's view, for example, I cannot say that

(5)   (The object) Elbert occurs in the fact that Elbert is passionate.

Now it would appear that I just *have* said it, but *on the Tractarian protosemantics* this is an illusion. For (5), like (2), will carve up according to the pattern

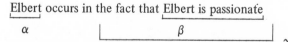

|_Elbert_| occurs in the fact that |_Elbert is passionate_|

    α |_____ β _____| γ

and, if true, must again allow us to parse γ as a designator (linguistic *object*) having β, a linguistic *fact*, as a part – which is impossible. (5), thus, is not a claim at all, on the Tractarian view, but rather ontological hash, for it putatively contains an object having a fact as one of its *parts*. And what is more, *any* attempt to *state* what is *shown* by the occurrence of the designator 'Elbert' in

(6)   Elbert is passionate

will collapse in exactly the same way. Thus what is shown *cannot* be said.

It is, therefore, Wittgenstein's protosemantic parsing of claims as facts which gives rise to the notorious ineffability doctrines of the *Tractatus*. In particular, I have argued, everything about language which we should *like* to state in a syntactic metalanguage becomes, on that parsing, ineffable as well. And so I now reject the Tractarian protosemantics. Claims are not linguistic facts but linguistic *objects*. They are, in fact, designators (and designator-pairs, etc.), in both language and metalanguage, and what is from the Tractarian standpoint ineffable can thus be effed with ease.

CHAPTER VII

THE PROTOSEMANTICS OF COMPLEX CLAIMS

In the preceding chapter, I sketched the protosemantics of *basic* claims — simple indicative declarative non-modal sentences in which all designators were proper names. I envisaged a representation of the world laid out in such claims — the Basic World Story — which was *ideally complete*. Each natural object was specifically protocorrelated with a natural linguistic object (designator-inscription) and non-linguistic objects of various kinds or characteristics were generically protocorrelated with designator-inscriptions of various kinds or characteristics in such a way that the resulting systems were extensionally isomorphic. It will be useful to look at this as the world story of an *omniscient* Author. Its most striking fictional posit is that *every object is named*, one name for each object. Whether it even makes sense to think of such a picture, given my earlier fusion of language with theory-writ-large, is one of the primary problems of this chapter. But before engaging this question, it will be useful to develop a view of truth-functions and, in the process, correct several oversimplifications and distortions.

1. TRUTH FUNCTIONS

The first thing which needs to be noticed is that, in outlining the fundamental protocorrelations, while I spoke of *isomorphism* what I actually sketched was a *homomorphism*. I said above that each non-linguistic object was protocorrelated with a natural linguistic object (designator-inscription). Given only what has gone before, however, this is inaccurate. So far, I have only outlined a correlation of non-linguistic objects with *sets* of designator inscriptions, for the inscription of 'Eunice' in

(1)   Eunice is pink

is numerically distinct from the inscription of 'Eunice' in

(2)   Eunice adores Albert.

On my protosemantic parsing, (1) is an R-pink* 'Eunice' and (2) is an LR-adores*# pair-object, ⟨'Eunice', 'Albert'⟩, having a 'Eunice' as one *com-*

ponent. The 'Eunice' which is a component of (2), however, is *not* R-pink*.
(It is, if you like, R-adores-Albert*.) Hence, it is not the 'Eunice' which constitutes (1). To give the protosemantic correlations in virtue of which (1) is
the claim that Eunice is pink, then, I ought correctly to write:

(1) designates Eunice (by being *a* 'Eunice') and claims of her that she is
pink (by being R-pink*), since 'Eunice's are protocorrelated with Eunice
and R-pink* designators with pink objects.

Here ' 'Eunice' ' enters *generically* as part of the predicate 'is *a* 'Eunice' '
which applies to such inscriptions as (1) and the first component of (2).

In an ideal protocorrelation, however, the isomorphism between the
system of representing objects and the system of represented objects which
was fraudulently presented in the preceding chapter as attained *would* be
complete. Designators would thus function in a way completely parallel to
indicators on a map. *One and the same dot* on a map, for example, is protocorrelated with — and thus indicates — Albany; is 5 mm in diameter (and
thus portrays Albany as being over 100,000 in population); is above the dot
indicating New York City (and thus portrays Albany as being to the north
of New York); is to the right of the dot protocorrelated with Buffalo; and
so on. In an ideal protocorrelation, similarly, the designator 'Eunice' which
was R-pink* would be *identical* to the designator 'Eunice' which was a component of the LR-adores*# designator-pair ⟨'Eunice', 'Albert'⟩, would also
be R-tall*, R-female*, a component of the LR-mother*# pair-object
⟨'Eunice', 'Gwendolyn'⟩, and of the LR-rebels-against*# pair ⟨'Gwendolyn',
'Eunice'⟩, and so on through all the empirical characteristics of and empirical relations among Eunice and other natural objects.

In a linear script, of course, this sort of system of representing objects is
impossible to achieve. A 'Eunice' which is R-pink* cannot also be R-tall*,
R-female*, and so on. And a 'Eunice' which is LR-mother* to a 'Gwendolyn' cannot also be, for example, RL-rebels-against* to that 'Gwendolyn'.
What we need, then, since we are limited in practice to a speech linear in
time and a script linear in space, is a set of devices for behaving *as if* we were
in fact able to produce the ideal isomorphic protocorrelations of an omniscient representer. The *basic* job of logical connectives and quantifiers is
to allow us to function cognitively *as if we were* ideal omniscient representers by permitting us to *anticipate* in the form of *recipes* the ideal protocorrelations of an omniscient representer not similarly limited. And this is
what is *formal* about formal logic. The apparatus of formal logic is content-
neutral in that it concerns only the relationship of simple representations
to composite representations quite independently of the subject matter

being represented. Thus, to take the clearest case, a *conjunction* of the form

F*a* & G*a*

(which I protosemantically parse as consisting of an L-F* '*a*' and an L-G* '*a*'
— i.e., an '*a*' having an 'F' to its left and an '*a*' having a 'G' to its left —
joined by an '&') points to (adumbrates) an ideal representation in which a
single designator, '*a*', would have a *pair* of counterpart characteristics corresponding respectively to our (linear) characteristics L-F* and L-G*.

We can get an intimation of how such a mode of representation would
work by envisioning a non-linear script, "Jumblese", of the sort sketched by
Sellars (*N&S*). Let us suppose that, for the Jumblese script, it is *italic*
designators which are protocorrelated with *red* objects as, in *our* script, it is
R-red* designators which are protocorrelated with red objects, and *boldface*
designators which are protocorrelated with *round* objects. Then what we
represent by writing

(3)   Hubert is red & Hubert is round

(or, equivalently: Hubert is red and round) will be represented by a single
'Hubert' inscription which is *both* italic *and* boldface, thus:

(4)   ***Hubert***

whereas 'Hubert is red' would be simply

Hubert

and 'Hubert is round',

Hubert

Analogously, for relations, in a non-linear script in which lusts-for-connec-
ted pair-objects are protocorrelated with pairs of designators the first of
which is *diagonally below and to the left of* the second, one would represent
what we write by

(5)   Ernestine lusts for Edward

(the LR-lusts*# pair-object (‘Ernestine’, ‘Edward’)) by the pair-object

(6)   Ernestine ^Edward.

If, now, one wished to say, for example, that Ernestine, who is red, lusts for
round Edward — which, in our script takes the form of a multiple conjunction:

(7)   Ernestine is red & Edward is round & Ernestine lusts for
           Edward

– in the Jumblese script, one could produce the complex inscription

(8)   *Ernestine* **Edward**

consisting of a diagonally-connected pair-object ⟨'Ernestine', 'Edward'⟩ the
first component of which is italic and the second boldface.

Conjunction of linear-script sentences thus anticipates what I shall call
conflation of protocorrelated basic claims – the combining of basic claims
representing parts of a world into a single total world-representing system.

Disjunction, too, anticipates the complete world-representation of an
omniscient representer. But where a conjunctive linear-script claim functions as a recipe enjoining the inclusion (by conflation) of counterparts of
both component claims in the ideal final representation, a disjunction of
linear-script claims anticipates an ideal final representation which includes
(as a whole includes its parts) the counterpart of *one or the other* (or, of
course, both) of the component claims.

With *negation* the situation is somewhat more complicated, as the classical
debate over negative facts (which lacks a parallel dispute over conjunctive or
disjunctive facts) might suggest. Protosemantically, we again have an anticipatory recipe. Here the root notion is a *prohibition*. Call a negated basic
claim a 'basic negation'. To assert a linear-script basic negation, then, is to
anticipate an ideal final representation which *excludes* the counterpart of
the basic claim negated. In this case, however, I must go on to say something about the *epistemology* of basic negations. What licenses the introduction of a conjunctive claim into the world-story is whatever licenses the
introduction individually of each of its components. But what licenses the
introduction of a basic negation into the world-story?

The issue has traditionally been engaged in the shadow of the classical
correspondence theory of truth. One proposal, championed by Russell, opts
for a correspondence theory of falsity as well:

A thing cannot be false except because of a fact, so that you find it extremely difficult
to say what exactly happens when you make a positive assertion that is false, unless
you are going to admit negative facts. (*PLA*, 214)

On Russell's view, a false basic claim is false by virtue of its *correspondence
in the false way* with a (real) negative fact, just as a true basic claim is true,
on his view, by virtue of its correspondence in the *true* way with a (real)
positive fact.

The essence of a proposition is that it can correspond in two ways with a fact, in what
one may call the true way or the false way... Supposing you have the proposition
'Socrates is mortal', either there would be the fact that Socrates is mortal or there

would be the fact that Socrates is not mortal. In the one case it corresponds in a way that makes the proposition true, in the other case in a way that makes the proposition false. (*PLA*, 208–9)

This view, of course, is beset with difficulties.[1] If one opts for a correspondence theory of falsity, however, there is no alternative but to posit a special relation of correspond*ence* and a special class of correspond*ants* to do the job. The only viable alternative, then, is to eschew the correspondence theory of falsity. And that, in turn, leaves us with two options.

On the first of these, we say that a basic claim is true if it corresponds to some (positive, atomic) fact; false, if it *fails* to correspond to *any* (positive, atomic) fact. The principal difficulty with this proposal is that it leaves falsity without an epistemology. For it seems that, in order to *discover* of a basic claim that it is false, one would have to canvass one by one each positive, atomic fact, noting in each case that the given basic claim fails appropriately to correspond.

It is to cope with this sort of consideration that the remaining proposal – what I shall call the *contrariety proposal* – has been advanced (originally by Demos). On this view (I quote Russell's exposition),

There is among propositions an ultimate relation of *opposition*; this relation is indefinable, but has the characteristic that when two propositions are opposites, they cannot both be true, though they may both be false. ...When we deny a proposition, what we are really doing is to assert: 'Some opposite of this proposition is true'. (*OP*, 288)

Now Russell correctly realizes that, so put, the contrariety proposal will not do the job for which it is intended – providing an ontological ground for a logical relation. For opposition is posited as a relation between propositions, and this is itself a relation *in dictu*, a logical relation, standing equally in need of a grounding *in re*. In *RNF*, I proposed an atomistic answer to this objection. It was, roughly, that properties and relations come in *families* such that (a) if some particulars *can* exemplify a property of relation from a given family, then they *do* exemplify some specific relation from that family, and (b) the properties or relations of a single family stand pairwise in a primitive (higher-order) relation of *exclusion*. To say of a basic claim, '$R_1(a_1, \ldots, a_n)$', that it is false, then, I suggested is to say that there is some other property or relation (of equal polyadicity) from the same family, F, as R_1 exemplified by the designated particulars:

$$\text{`}R_1(a_1, \ldots, a_n)\text{' is false} =$$
$$(\exists F)(\exists R_2)[R_1, R_2 \,\epsilon\, F \,\&\, R_2(a_1, \ldots, a_n)]$$

Now in the current work, I have, of course, eschewed both an ontology of facts and Russellian-style Platonism with respect to properties and relations, relocating the fundamental insights of the correspondence theory of truth in a protocorrelational grounding for representations arising out of a pragmatist view of truth as assertibility in accordance with the content rules of a language. Can anything, then, be made of the classical question of negation within this distinctly non-classical framework?

I think so. The traditional problem of an ontological grounding for logical relations becomes, as I see it, the problem of the epistemological fundamentum for acceptance of claims making essential use of those relations. In particular, the traditional problem of negation which gave rise to the dialectic which I have just sketched becomes the problem of specifying *language entries* for true basic negations. How do I come to be in the position to accept (occupy a position corresponding to) a basic negation?

Language entries, I have argued, are essentially linguistic responses to non-linguistic stimuli. And I suggested, further, that nothing in principle stands in the way of entering the inferential network of claims constitutive of a linguistic representation of the world at *any* point. I think, however, that the classical dialectic of negation demands a modification of this stance. For while, for example, pink Eunice can be − simply *qua* pink − an appropriate stimulus for eliciting 'Eunice is pink', Eunice who is not, for example, yellow is not − *simply as not being yellow* − an appropriate stimulus for eliciting 'Eunice is not yellow'. For Eunice is also not green, not blue, not invisible, not hexagonal, not a fish, and so on indefinitely − and there is nothing in the case to *select* the *cognitive* item 'yellow' for explicit denial. I conclude, then, that to arrive at 'Eunice is not yellow' *requires an inferential step.*

Where classically one speaks of families of Platonistic qualia, I have spoken instead of linguistic items constituted by (implicitly defined by) sets of content rules of inference. What corresponds, initially, to a family of pairwise exclusive determinates under a single determinable, then, is, in first approximation, a family of *basic content rules* licensing non-enthymematically such inferences as

> Eunice is pink
> Therefore, Eunice is not yellow

or, as an example of higher polyadicity,

> Albany is north of New York
> Therefore, Albany is not south of New York.

These rules will be inferential *permissions*. But I have already argued that the root protocorrelational notion of negation is that of a *prohibition* − the injunction to exclude a representation of a specified sort from the ideal final representation of the world. Thus, finally, I wish to suggest that these content rules are, in turn, derivative from a still more basic level at which a family of linguistic items is partially constituted by a system of *prohibitive* rules in which the notion of *negation* does not appear. Thus, crudely, for example:

<u>Eunice is pink</u>
Prohibited therefore,   Eunice is green
                        Eunice is yellow
                        Eunice is blue
                                •
                                •
                                •

As the extensional counterpart of a permissive content rule is facilitated inscriptional behavior — an *elicited* linguistic response to a linguistic stimulus — the extensional counterpart of a *prohibitive* content rule will be *impeded* inscriptional behavior — the *inhibition* of certain linguistic responses to certain linguistic stimuli. The concept of negation, then, may be viewed as implicitly constituted by a single superadded inferential rule which transforms a given prohibition into a counterpart permission:

<u>Prohibited: S</u>
Permitted therefore, not-S.

It is these systems of prohibitive content rules and their extensional cash as inhibitions of linguistic (ideally, inscriptional) behavior in response to linguistic stimuli which form the counterpart in my non-classical framework of the Platonistic higher-order primitive relation of *exclusion* among properties or relations of a family and which constitute the ultimate ground of negation by facilitating entry, now two steps removed, to a position in the inferential network corresponding to a true basic negation. And if this is correct, the structuring of predicates into families of pairwise exclusive determinates under common determinables is, as I hypothesized in *RNF*, not merely a local and adventitious feature of our language but, indeed, a necessary precondition of the possession of a language in which negation is possible at all.

These observations in hand, I can make good too a small epistemological hiatus in my discussions earlier in this chapter by pointing out that *disjunctive* claims admit of entry, first, from either (or both) of the disjuncts:

<u>p</u>   <u>q</u>
Therefore, p or q   Therefore, p or q

but also, second, in DeMorgan style from the negation of the conjunction of the negated disjuncts:

> <u>not (not p and not q)</u>
> Therefore, p or q

It is this latter option which makes it possible for us to be in the position warrantedly to accept a disjunction although not similarly licensed to accept either disjunct.[2]

The traditional Laws of Thought (Identity, Excluded Middle, and Non-Contradiction) emerge from this point of view as the reflections of fundamental *deontic* principles;

Identity: A move which is permitted is permitted.

Excluded Middle: A move is either permitted or prohibited.

Non-Contradiction: No move is both permitted and prohibited.

And what controls such systems of deontic principles is the impetus to a system of rules which is *executable*. Permissions having as extensional counterpart behavioral facilitation and prohibitions, behavioral inhibition, a system of rules failing to be consonant with *such* deontic principles would be a system of rules which *could not* be collectively obeyed.[3]

2. QUANTIFICATION

Ramsey, considering the relation between quantified claims and truth-functionally compound claims, makes the following observations:

> (x). φx differs from a conjunction because

(a)	It cannot be written out as one.
(b)	Its constitution as a conjunction is never used; we never use it in class-thinking except in its application to a finite class, i.e., we use only the applicative rule.
(c)	...It always goes beyond what we know or want; cf. Mill on 'All men are mortal' and 'The Duke of Wellington is mortal'. It expresses an inference we are at any time prepared to make, not a belief of the primary sort...
(d)	The relevant degree of certainty is the certainty of the particular case, or of a finite set of particular cases; not of an infinite number which we never use, and of which we couldn't be certain at all.

> (x) . φx resembles a conjunction

(a)	In that it contains all lesser, i.e., here all finite, conjunctions, and appears as a sort of infinite product.
(b)	When we ask what would make it true, we inevitably answer that it is true if and only if every x has φ; i.e., when we regard it as a proposition capable of the two cases truth and falsity, we are forced to make it a conjunction, and to have a theory of conjunctions which we cannot express for lack of symbolic power. (*FM*, 237–8)

Now there is much that is provocative in these comparisons, and a fully developed and well-rounded discussion of quantification would need to examine them in considerable detail, but I have space here for only a schematic treatment. So I shall be brief and, I fear, somewhat dogmatic in consequence.

In the first place, what needs to be done is to rigidly enforce the separation of epistemological and protosemantical questions. Thus (c) and (d) – and perhaps (b) – of Ramsey's canvassed *differences* address essentially epistemological questions. They are concerned with *entries* to positions in the inferential network which correspond to quantified claims and, more remotely, with the degree of confidence which we may place in such a claim grounded by a particular finite set of evidences. Now I am convinced that the universally quantified claims which we actually come to *accept* are uniformly counterpart conditionals of material rules of inference, and, since I have had much to say earlier concerning the adoption of material rules and the process traditionally thought of as inductive generalization, I shall not further address these epistemological issues here. (a) of the differences, (a) and (b) of the resemblances, and, to some extent, (b) of the differences as well, however, concern properly protosemantic questions and, thus, demand some attention here.

The protosemantic thesis which I have adopted is that the apparatus of formal logic permits us to conduct our cognitive life *as if* in possession of the ideal final world-representation by anticipating that representation in the form of recipes for its construction. And this holds true for the quantificational apparatus of language as well as for its truth-functional apparatus. From the viewpoint of our ideal omniscient representer, the difference which Ramsey marks as (a) does not obtain, for we have adopted in his case a fiction, that *every object has a name*. In the ideal final representation of a world in which, as *we* would say, '(x)Fx' is true, each designator would have a representational property counterpart to our L-F* (having an 'F' to the left) and thereby claim of the object designated that it is F. *Our* use of the universal quantifier anticipates this ideal final representation, in effect, by enjoining as a recipe its construction.

For a finite universe, then, quantification offers no difficulty in principle. What complicates matters, of course, is the envisaged possibility of a world containing an infinite number of objects. If that is the case, a quantified claim anticipating the conflation of an *infinite* number of basic claims of a form must do something more. Since basic claims *are* designators, it must anticipate not merely the claiming of each designated object that it is, say, F, but the *designation of the objects as well*. I want, in other words, to take seriously Ramsey's notion that we have in universal quantification "a theory of conjunctions which we cannot express for lack of symbolic power" and to suggest that our use of quantified claims is *doubly* anticipatory. It anticipates, first, the conflation in an ideal final representation of an infinite number of basic claims of a given form. But it anticipates, in addition – and, in an important sense, *primarily* – the enrichment of our current symbolic powers to the point where we would be able in principle to make each of these basic claims singly. That is, it anticipates an infinity of designators.

Now what would this "ability in principle" amount to? In what sense of 'have' could *we have* an infinite number of designators? Well, this is not the place for an exhaustive study of the notion of the infinite, so I shall simply assert what, on another occasion, I may hope to defend in detail. The only way in which *we* could "have" an infinite number of designators is by having (now in the literal sense of 'have') *mastery of a technique for producing designators according to a rule.*

The view I adopt here is essentially Tractarian. Wittgenstein writes (*TLP*, 5.521):

> I dissociate the concept *all* from truth-functions.
> Frege and Russell introduced generality in association with logical product or logical sum. This made it difficult to understand the propositions '(∃x).fx' and '(x).fx', in which both ideas are embedded.

Wittgenstein wishes to distinguish the *mode of composition of basic claims* (conjunctive in the case of universal quantifiers, disjunctive in the case of existential quantifiers) anticipated by a quantified claim from the *specification of the arguments* (basic claims) to be thus composed. What is unique about quantified claims is that they specify the basic claims the composition of which they anticipate not by enumeration, as do finite conjunctions and disjunctions, but by means of a propositional function. On my view, however, basic claims *are* designators and so, for me, there are *three* aspects of the anticipated ideal final representation embodied in a here-and-now quantified claim. First, there is the adumbrated mode of composition; second, an indication of the appropriate character of the designators appearing in the final representation in virtue of which each claims of the object which it designates that it is, say, F (i.e., that characteristic in the ideal final representation which is the counterpart of our L-F*); and, finally, the specification of the designators themselves. Wittgenstein envisions the specification of basic claim truth-arguments by means of a propositional function. Since, on my view, basic claims are designators having certain empirical characteristics, the use of a quantified claim anticipates both the representing characteristic of designators in an ideal final representation and the construction of the designators themselves constitutive of that representation according to a rule.

From this point of view, the current debate between advocates of an "objectual" interpretation of quantifiers (e.g., Quine) and advocates of a "substitutional" interpretation of quantifiers (e.g., Marcus) is seen to be devoid of substance. For the present use of quantified claims is now seen as an *anticipation* of an ideal final representation in which the "objectual" and "substitutional" truth-conditions would, in extension, *necessarily coincide*. And what quantification permits us to do is to conduct ourselves cognitively *as if* this envisaged ideal coincidence were here-and-now fact.

What is particularly surprising is to discover that intimations of a representation of the world in which designators *are* constructible according to a rule are already peering over the epistemological horizon. Representational language, I have argued, is — epistemologically — physical theory writ large. What is suggestive is that some contemporary physicists, impressed by what current theory posits as the intrinsic qualitative indistinguishability of electrons, have already begun to make a subtle shift in their conceptual scheme. They are beginning to speak of *regions of space* as being 2-electron regions, 5-electron regions, and so on, transforming what are currently logical subjects of extrinsic qualitative and relational predications (electrons) into logical predicates of regions of space *designated by coordinate names*. And a *coordinate* designator is, precisely, the sort of designator which admits of construction according to a rule (although possibly, as relativity theory has taught us, a very complex one).

I have, unfortunately, had space here only for the most schematic treatment of some of the manifold complications which must be introduced into the picture of representation arising from consideration of the Basic World Story before it begins to make full and effective contact with those languages which we in fact speak. Simply to list what I have been forced to omit would consume nearly as much space again as what I have been able to include.[4] But the broad outlines of my account should now be clear. Rather than engage the details of accommodation between my general theorizing and the particularities of everyday speech, then, I should like to conclude by moving my picture onto a larger metaphysical canvas. For my remarks have throughout presupposed a metaphysical realism, which realism itself, as I intimated in my earlier remarks on the Principle of Charity, has recently been opened to significant challenge. I shall conclude, then, with a discussion of the way in which a theory of representation fits into a full realistic metaphysic and, if I am successful, with the lineaments of a defense of the realistic stance itself as well.

CHAPTER VIII

REPRESENTATION AND MAN

The neo-Kantian revolution in reaction to the Humean excesses of atomism, positivism, and phenomenalism characteristic of the early parts of this century has now been in full flower for some time.[1] One attuned to the historical dialectics of philosophy, then, should have been anticipating a neo-Hegelian counter-reaction for several years. Nor would he have been disappointed. Indeed, the lines of battle have recently been well and sharply drawn in Rorty's manifesto "The World Well Lost".

Rorty conducts his argument against the background of a critique of transcendental arguments which establishes them to be essentially verificationist in structure and, thus, essentially anti-skeptical (and negative) in import.[2] That access to the reality of *noumena* is thus held to be blocked, and Rorty proposes to block any other as well by an argument which combines two contemporary themes to arrive at what he takes to be a decisive criticism of the notion of *alternative conceptual frameworks* and what he holds to be correlative to it, the "realist's" notion of a *world*. Both of these contemporary themes have emerged in the course of the present study. The first is an attack on the notion of an empirical *given*, broadly characteristic of recent philosophy.[3] If this attack is sound, Rorty argues, the Kantian distinction between receptivity and spontaneity evaporates before it as well:

> The possibility of different conceptual schemes highlights the fact that a Kantian unsynthesized intuition can exert no influence on how it is to be synthesized – or, at best, can exert only an influence we shall have to describe in a way as relative to a chosen conceptual scheme as our description of everything else. Insofar as a Kantian intuition is effable, it is just a perceptual judgment, and thus not *merely* "intuitive". Insofar as it is ineffable, it is incapable of having an explanatory function.

> The Kantian point that different a priori concepts would, if there could be such things, give us a different phenomenal world gives place either to the straightforward but paradoxical claim that different concepts give us different worlds, or to dropping the notion of "conceptual framework" altogether. 'Phenomenal' can no longer be given a sense, once Kantian "intuitions" drop out. (*WWL*, 650)

The second theme is implicit in the Quinean arguments for indeterminacy of translation and inscrutability of reference which I discussed in earlier chapters. It arises out of a general critique of the "philosophical sense of 'meaning' " and manifests itself variously as an attack upon the analytic/synthetic distinction, a correlative criticism of the necessary/contingent distinction, and a consequent collapsing of the notion of a conceptual framework — putatively constituted by a set of synthetic and necessary concepts — into the general notion of an empirical theory.

> Once the necessary is identified with the analytic and the analytic is explicated in terms of meaning, an attack on the notion of... the "philosophical" sense of 'meaning' becomes an attack on the notion of a "conceptual framework" in any sense that assumes a distinction of kind between this notion and that of "empirical theory". (*WWL*, 651–2)

Now in adopting a view of perceptual judgments as linguistic responses to non-linguistic stimuli, I have firmly taken my stand in opposition to the notion of an empirical given. The test of a theory, I have argued, is its *explanatory* power, not its consonance with semantically structured yet preconceptual data, and explanatory power, in turn, cashes out in terms of the increasing scope, integration, and coherence of an inferential structure, admitting of *re*descriptions of phenomena already entering conceptual consciousness under some description contributed by the perceiver. In addition, while taking a stand against the Quinean critique of meaning in general, I accepted as well the assimilation of "conceptual framework" to "empirical theory" which Rorty takes to be the second prong of his attack upon the notion of alternative conceptual frameworks and thus upon the notion of a world.

Yet, on the other hand, my stance throughout this study has been realistic *au fond*, and, indeed, "scientific realism" played a *premissory* role, along with the rejection of the given, in my argument which *led* to the assimilation of alternative conceptual frameworks (*qua* alternative languages) to alternative empirical theories. Rorty, in contrast, believes that the two anti-Kantian themes which we share can be worked up into an argument dictating the abandoning of the "realist" doctrine that "the world" could turn out to be *radically different* from what we now conceive it to be. As he parses "realism", the truths expressed by "persons using a conceptual scheme different from our own" would be expressed in "a language not translatable into our own" (*WWL*, 652) — and that, he argues, is a vacuous notion. It follows that the vast majority of our *present* beliefs about the world must be true. As this conclusion stands in direct contradiction to my own, it is important that we take a more detailed look at the argument which Rorty offers in support of it.

The key is Quine's rejection of the notion of meaning as anything over and above "what is contextually defined in predicting the foreigner's behavior" (*WWL*, 653). For, if we follow Quine here, Rorty argues – and he takes Quine's arguments for that rejection to be compelling – we shall no longer be able to fund a distinction between an *untranslatable* language and *no language at all.*

Once we imagine different ways of carving up the world, nothing could stop us from attributing "untranslatable languages" to *anything* that emits a variety of signals. (*WWL*, 653)

The crunch comes when this line of thought is applied to a hypothetical foreigner who is a member of a future community of our own sophisticated descendants. Hypothesize, proposes Rorty, a Galactic civilization of the future populated by persons holding so radically different a view of the world from our own that their language is in principle untranslatable into English. They "carve up the world according to a radically different conceptual scheme".

A Galactic time-traveler come among us, we now realize, would eventually be forced to abandon his original presumption that we were persons when he failed to correlate our utterances with our environment in any way that enabled him to construct an English-Galactic lexicon. Our initial assumption that the Galactic emissary was a person would be frustrated by the same sort of discovery. (*WWL*, 657)

But then,

... for all we know, our *contemporary* world is filled with unrecognizable persons. Why should we ignore the possibility that the trees and the bats and the butterflies all have their various untranslatable languages in which they are busily expressing their beliefs and desires to one another?

Let the notion of a person be as complex and multiply criterioned as you please, still I do not think that it will come unstuck from that of a complex interlocked set of beliefs and desires, nor that the latter notion can be separated from that of the potentiality for translatable speech. So I think that to rule the butterflies out is to rule out the Galactics and the Neanderthals, and that to allow extrapolation to the latter is to allow for the possibility that the very same beliefs and desires which our Galactic descendants will hold are being held even now by the butterflies. We can dig in our heels and say that terms like 'person', 'belief', 'desire', and 'language' are ultimately as token-reflexive as 'here' and 'now' or 'morally right', so that in each case essential reference is made to where *we* are. But that will be the *only* way of ruling out the Galactic, and thus the *only* way of ruling out the butterfly. (*WWL*, 657–8)

The upshot, for Rorty, is that in the only *non-vacuous* sense which can be made of the notion of a "world which *determines* the truth", "the world" is just "whatever that vast majority of our beliefs not currently in question are currently thought to be about" (*WWL*, 662). For, if any possible language must, to count as a *language* at all, be translatable into our own, it follows that the vast majority of our *current* beliefs must be true. Consequently,

... "the world" will just be the stars, the people, the tables, and the grass – all those things which nobody except the occasional "scientific realist" philosopher thinks might not exist. The fact that the vast majority of our beliefs must be true will, on this view, guarantee the existence of the vast majority of the things we now think we are talking about. (*WWL*, 662)

What must be abandoned, in contrast, is the notion of "the world" as an *independent* reality as used in such phrases as "different conceptual schemes carve up the world differently".

"Truth" in the sense of "truth taken apart from any theory" and "world" taken as "what determines such truth" are notions that were... made for each other. Neither can survive apart from the other. (*WWL*, 663)

Thus, if the notion of "alternative conceptual frameworks" disappears, the correlative realist notion of "the world" disappears with it.

"The world" is either the purely vacuous notion of the ineffable cause of sense and goal of intellect [and thus no genuine notion at all], or else a name for the objects that inquiry at the moment is leaving alone... (*WWL*, 663)

The catch, of course, is that, if Rorty is correct, the vast majority of what inquiry *at the moment* is leaving alone, it must continue to leave alone *forevermore*.

Where I part company with Rorty is neither on the question of an empirical given (for we both reject the notion) nor on the assimilation of "alternative conceptual frameworks" to "empirical theories" (for we both accept the identification). Nor are we in disagreement with regard to putative languages of the butterflies. Indeed, I am prepared to go even further with Rorty and assent to his claim that the notion of a pair of languages which are *mutually* untranslatable into one another is a vacuous notion. Where Rorty has not made his case, I think, is in his claim that English and Galactic would constitute *such* a pair of languages.

In fact, as I have delineated the constraints of the epistemology of scientific inquiry, they cannot be so related. For the prime desideratum of a successor theory, I argued, is that it explain the descriptive successes of its predecessor(s). Such explanation, I claimed, paradigmatically takes the form of modeling by counterpart concepts the predecessor(s) within the successor, establishing thereby the predecessor descriptions to be both literally false and approximately true, from the descriptive standpoint of the successor theory. And for this to be possible, it follows that *the language of the predecessor theory must be in principle translatable into the language of the successor theory*. In the case in point, in particular, if Galactic is in fact an epistemologically well-grounded evolutionary successor framework to our own, English *will* be translatable into it. The converse, of course, need not be true – any more than it must be possible to translate our talk about quantum mechanics into Ancient Greek or Navajo in order for the latter pair to qualify as languages.

But while translatability of Galactic into English is not a requirement for Galactic's being a language, *learnability* of Galactic by English-speakers *is*. What will be the case, of course, is that Galactic cannot be learned as one typically learns a *second* language, that is, *by* learning to translate Galactic locutions into our native tongue. Rather, Galactic must be learnable by us as it is learned by *its* native speakers, as a (second, in our case) *native* language. And it is precisely here that the Galactics part company from the butter-flies. Only if one implicitly espouses a view which equates language-learning with *translation* of the target language into a (perhaps innate) language already possessed will the *non-learnability* of Galactic by English-speakers be thought of as a consequence of the *non-translatability* of Galactic into English. And, of course, Quine and Rorty both are no less anxious to reject *that* model of language-learning than I am.

On the position for which I have been arguing, then, it does make sense to speak of a world over and above "the objects which inquiry is at the moment leaving alone" – a world of which continuing scientific theorizing gives an increasingly more adequate picture, ideal consonance with which would constitute the truth of representations in a limiting sense. But, as I Peirceanly characterize the world just *as* what is represented by the ideal limit of scientific theorizing, there is more to my brand of realism than "the purely vacuous notion of the ineffable cause of sense and goal of intellect". On the realism which I espouse, on the contrary, the world is in principle effable. What continuing application of the scientific method gives us pre-cisely is an increasingly adequate representation *of things in themselves*. All this would be pointless, of course, if the notion of a limit of scientific theo-rizing could not be non-metaphorically funded from our position here and now. But, while we cannot of course now *say* what would be represented by scientific inquiry carried to its ideal limit – just as we cannot now say what *will* be represented by the (inevitable) successors to our *currently* best-grounded explanatory theories – it was one of the central burdens of Chap-ter V to argue that we can *now* make non-metaphorical sense of inquiry *tend-ing* toward a limit-representation, i.e., of theoretical convergence.

Rorty holds that to reject the notion of an empirical given and to assimi-late conceptual frameworks to empirical theories is to abandon as well the

notion of "truth taken apart from any theory". And with this I would
agree, provided it be properly parsed. For it is one thing to hold, as I do,
that the notion of empirical truth is necessarily conceptually tied to the *process* of empirical theorizing, and quite another to hold, as Rorty does, that
empirical truth is necessarily and forever pinned to some *particular* scheme
or system of concepts. Rorty's "realist" would cut truth free of theorizing
überhaupt. And this I agree is impossible, for the *sense* of 'true', I argued, is
assertibility in accordance with linguistic rules – and the content rules of a
language *are*, epistemologically, the material rules of a theory. But while
correspondence cannot be the *test* of truth, it is a consequence of my arguments that truth in the limit *consists in* an ideal isomorphism between representing system and represented world. It is precisely by treating (ideal) truth
as a *limit* concept that one can avoid both the Scylla of *unknowable* classical correspondence independent of theorizing in general, as espoused by
Rorty's "realist", and the Charybdis of viewing (ideal) truth as consilience
with a *particular* set of concepts deployed by us here and now, as espoused
by Rorty himself. The ideal truth is thus *neither* already known *nor* ultimately unknowable. The correct thing to say about it is "We're heading in
that direction".

I have characterized Rorty's view as, implicitly at least, neo-Hegelian.
Rorty himself thinks of it as a purified revival of Dewey's "naturalized"
Hegelian historicism.

> In this historicist vision, the arts, the sciences, the sense of right and wrong, and the
> institutions of society are not attempts to embody or formulate truth or goodness or
> beauty. They are attempts to solve problems – to modify our beliefs and desires and
> activities in ways that will bring us greater happiness than we have now. (*WWL*, 665)

Now I want to take seriously the question to which Rorty here (and Dewey
before him) offers an answer. In the framework for which I have been
arguing, it comes to this: People seek explanations. The search for increasingly coherent explanatory theories is the motive force underlying, and
encapsulates the epistemic end of, scientific inquiry in particular and, as I
have argued, empirical inquiry in general. Explanation, in turn, cashes out as
redescription. The search for explanations is the search for increasingly
broad, integrated, and coherent inferential systems constitutive of families
of concepts in terms of which the continuing flux of experience can be ever
more adequately described. But why do people seek thus to represent the
world? Why do people have the epistemic ends which they in fact have and
which give rise to a series of increasingly adequate representations? This is
the question which I wish finally to engage.

The initial reaction will surely be to reject the question. We can appropriately ask, it will be said, of any particular person why *he* seeks certain
explanations, but there is no sense to be made of the question of why
people in general seek explanations. For any individual person, perhaps, a
psychoanalytic account might be given of why he has and pursues the ends
with which we find him, but there is no *more general* account to be given of
why *people* have and pursue the ends with which we find them.

Now I think that this reaction to the question is a mistake. And it is a
mistake for reasons over and above its being an instance of epistemological
obstructionism – "blocking the road to inquiry", as Peirce put it. It is a
mistake because the presumptive evidence concerning people is contrary to
a presupposition of the rejection. To reject the question on these grounds is
to presuppose that the "will to explain" is an idiosyncratic feature of
isolated persons or groups of persons – say, "the scientists". But this is incorrect. As I have argued earlier, *all* empirical reasoning is in essence abductive, whether it be the sophisticated theorizing of the quantum physicist or
the primitive tale-telling of the Australian aborigines. From the elemental
mythologies of primitive man to contemporary postulational microphysics
is a great distance measured in terms of sophistication. But *epistemologically* myth and microtheory are brothers, and equally close kin to the tentative explanatory posits of a businessman trying to start his balky automobile on a cold winter morning. Each is a system of claims and principles
of inference accepted because it provides, *at the time of its acceptance*, the
best available explanatory account of a range of phenomena, that is, because
it permits those phenomena to be redescribed in a way which subsumes
them under concepts constituted by a single, integrated, coherent inferential
system. While the nature and sophistication of the particular explanatory
accounts may vary widely from individual to individual and from culture to
culture, the *presence* of explanatory accounts is a human invariant. The
search for explanations and the consequent evolving development of an increasingly richer representation of the world is a characteristic, not of isolated individuals or groups of individuals, but of man *as a species*. That
people's systems of beliefs and representations of the world grow out of and
are controlled by the ends of explanation is too pervasive and essential a
feature of human life to be dismissed as a brute and unexplainable fact.

On the other hand, the contrasting initial reaction that men seek explanations simply because they wish to *understand* their world must also be dismissed. Not, however, because it is mistaken. Rather it is all *too* true. For,
as I have noted earlier, the connexion between explanation and understanding is analytic. We understand *only* what we can explain, and the process

of explaining a range of phenomena *is* the process of coming to understand those phenomena. The most that this response offers us, then, is a rephrasal of the original question: Why do people seek to understand the world?

Rorty (like Dewey before him) takes neither of these false paths. Rather he sees the question for the legitimate inquiry which it is, and he offers an appropriately sophisticated answer: Empirical inquiry is an activity in the service of higher ends. The ends of understanding (explanation by means of increasingly adequate representation) are, indeed, the ultimate ends controlling the enterprise of *inquiry*, but inquiry itself, viewed more broadly, must be seen as but a *means* to a more fundamental end – the achieving of human happiness, of "the good life for man". What we do not understand, the argument runs, we can neither predict nor control. Consequently, only when we understand the world can we act most effectively (can we so adjust our behavior) to optimize all those factors which conduce to the good life for man. The epistemic ends-in-view of understanding must thus be seen as merely *proximate* ends. From a broader perspective, the belief-systems and representations generated by inquiry are means or instruments only for the attaining of the genuinely ultimate ends of *all* human activity – society, art, and morality, as well as empirical inquiry – the ends of human happiness.

This one might fairly call "epistemological instrumentalism". Although it is an initially attractive position, we must, I believe, in the end pass beyond it also. For epistemological instrumentalism mislocates the relationship between understanding and human happiness. There is, to be sure, a necessary connexion. But it is not the connexion between necessary means and autonomous end. It is a connexion even more intimate. For understanding is an *essential part* of the good life for man. The relation of human understanding to human happiness is not like the relation between buying an automobile and owning it. It is much more like the relation between eating an apple and enjoying it. The activity is a constituent of the enjoyment; it is *eating the apple* which we enjoy. Put somewhat archaically, the enjoyment is *supervenient* upon the eating, not consequent upon it as effect upon cause nor separable from it as end from means. Human understanding and the good life for man are related in *that* way. Happiness is not separable from nor consequent upon understanding, but rather supervenient upon it. Understanding is itself a wholly autonomous human good. It is thus not merely a precondition of human happiness but rather a prime constituent of that happiness. In the end, then, epistemological instrumentalism will not do.

And what course, then, is left for us? The only remaining alternative, as I see it, is to begin to take Aristotle seriously: "Every man *by nature* desires to know." What I propose is that we view the present quest for an explanation of human epistemic activity as another proper *empirical* question. *It thus becomes a question which falls within the legitimate scope of that enterprise which it itself proposes that we undertake to explain.* Thereby we turn the methodology back upon itself as subject. And this, in turn, gives a radical twist to the problem.

What we have been seeking is an explanation of why, with respect to his activities giving rise to an increasingly richer and more adequate representation of the world, man is as he is. Taken seriously, the Aristotelian proposal suggests that men seek to understand and thus to represent the world as a matter of *natural* necessity. It is, crudely, a law of nature that man, as a species, seeks explanations of phenomena and thereby comes to project increasingly adequate representations of his world. Since it is the job of empirical science to develop coherent theoretical frameworks which provide explanatory accounts of natural laws, it now becomes a part of that enterprise to develop a comprehensive theoretical account of man-in-the-universe from which it will follow that men seek to understand and represent the universe of which they are a part. And the only way to do *this*, in turn, requires that we take seriously the fact − for it is a fact − that we are evolutionary *products* of, and a *subsystem* of, the very universe which we undertake ever more adequately to represent.

What I am suggesting is a shift in perspective tantamount to Kant's "Copernican revolution". We can understand our representational activities, I propose, only by redescribing them in terms of the concepts of a *total* theory of the universe as a physical system which, of natural necessity, evolves subsystems which in turn necessarily project increasingly adequate representations of the whole. To put it crudely, we must come to see the physical universe as an integrated physical system which necessarily "grows knowers" and which thereby comes to mirror itself within itself. Such a theory treats man and the universe as explanatorily *correlative* by assimilating them to a single inferential framework. The fundamental nature of man would, of course, be explained by an appeal to the general character of the physical universe of and within which man is an evolutionary product. But, equally, the fundamental nature of the universe would be explained by showing that *only* in a universe of that *sort* (where the sort is now to be specified in precise and quantitative terms) *could* there evolve a species of entities which generate representations of the total physical system of which they are a part and thereby *come to inquire* into the fundamental nature of that system. We cannot understand ourselves and our epistemology, in other words, until we understand them both as products of an evolving physical universe and as parts of the very process of its evolution. And we cannot understand the physical universe until we have a representation of it precisely *as* a physical system such that, within it, a species of entities necessarily evolves which seeks to understand and represent it.[4]

I opened this chapter with neo-Hegelian anticipations. We can now see that the picture of man-in-the-universe which I have been adumbrating is, in a sense, a fulfillment of these expectations. For the universe thus conceived as an intelligible total system evolving *within* itself a representation *of* itself models nicely Hegel's conception of the Absolute evolving to self-consciousness. In *Die Phänomenologie des Geistes*, Hegel proposes that we identify subject-matter and method, viewing the history of philosophy as the history of consciousness, its method as the dialectic of consciousness, and the goal of philosophical inquiry as the coming of consciousness to an awareness of its evolutionary history and, thus, to an awareness of itself as consciousness – to self-consciousness. This, too, finds a parallel in the view which I have been sketching. For in treating the having by us of a representation-yielding methodology of empirical inquiry as itself a fit subject for empirical inquiry, I perform also the reflexive trick of ultimately identifying subject and method. And the upshot is the same, for what emerges in Hegel's philosophy as the self-actualization of the Absolute finds its parallel here in a synoptic empirical theory of man-in-the-universe which views the epistemic activities of persons and the fundamental nature of the physical arena in which those activities occur as explanatorily correlative, neither being understandable apart from a conception of the other. When we ask *whose* theory this (ultimate) theory would be, however, it becomes equally appropriate to assign it to the universe as subject as to ourselves – for it is precisely a theory which posits us and our representations as necessary products of the natural evolution of that universe. We are, aphoristically speaking, the universe's way of asking itself what it is like. And in this way, the traditional dichotomy between knowing subject and known object at last disappears.

It is this dichotomy which Hegel's idealism addresses. The fatal flaw of Kantianism was, and remains, the notion of epistemologically inaccessible *noumena* – the ineffable things-in-themselves. Once a wedge is driven between experience and objects, once the possibility is raised that objects might not conform to our representations of them, the long but quick slide to skepticism and, ultimately, solipsism is begun. Kant, in his "Refutation of Idealism", attempted to bridge this gap by arguing that all experience, being subsumable under *a priori* concepts contributed by us, is necessarily of objects. But, at the end of his inquiry, stepping back from the first-person point of view, he introduces the possibility that *our* set of *a priori*

concepts is but one of a possible many. Thus, while holding that it is necessary that I *experience* objects in accordance with the conditions which I
impose in my *a priori* synthesis of intuitions, Kant is nevertheless able to ask
whether it is possible that *objects themselves* do not obey these conditions.

In this light, Hegel's contribution can be seen as a recognition of the illegi-
timacy of this question *from the first-person point of view*. For, from that
point of view, there is no way to intelligibly talk about, point to, or otherwise indicate a world of objects beyond our possible knowledge. This
Wittgenstein recognizes as well (*TLP*, 5.61):

> Logic pervades the world: the limits of the world are also its limits.
> So we cannot say in logic, 'The world has this in it, and this, but not that.'
> For that would appear to presuppose that we were excluding certain possibilities, and
> this cannot be the case, since it would require that logic should go beyond the limits of
> the world; for only in that way could it view those limits from the other side as well.
> We cannot think what we cannot think; so what we cannot think we cannot *say*
> either.

If, then, we hew consistently to the first-person point of view, *the* world
becomes, as Wittgenstein recognized, *my* world. (*TLP*, 5.62) The dichotomy
between knower and known can be overcome, but there is a price. For
Wittgenstein, the price is a doctrine of ineffability; for Hegel, it is idealism.
Objective knowledge becomes possible, for Hegel, but only because the
world is an aspect of the knower. In the last analysis, the objective is seen to
be subjective after all. Ultimately, then, *all* knowledge is *self*-knowledge, because ultimately there is nothing else to know.

The alternative is to naturalize our epistemology and to abandon the first-
person viewpoint *au fond*. This is the pragmatist thrust, but it is difficult to
carry through consistently. Quine and Rorty, as we have seen, attempt the
gambit. But, failing to get a clear view of empirical epistemology as abductive and thus as *presupposing* realism, they succeed at best in going plural,
but not public. Quine emerges in linguistic solipsism of the present idiolect,
and Rorty, while he does better, in the end substitutes for the classical
solipsistic identification of *the* world with *my* world only a pluralized
version which identifies *the* world with *ours*.

The picture which I have presented, on the other hand, is naturalized
through and through. For empirical epistemology, I have argued, is to be
seen from an *external* point of view as the continual causal shaping of a
system of representations *within* the represented world and *by* it. Thus, ultimately, the dichotomy between knower and known is overcome here too.
But it is not by the idealistic assimilation of the known object to the
knowing subject. Rather it is the knower who is assimilated to the known.

For a consistent naturalism sees us and our representations as both *parts* of and causal and evolutionary *products* of that world which we come ever more adequately to represent. And in the end, then, we and our world come together. For the whole is mirrored in the part which we are, but it is mirrored precisely *as* a whole which *necessarily* evolves this part which thus mirrors it.

Hegel, then, was wrong — but not so far wrong. He was wrong in attempting to overcome the dichotomy between experience and things-in-themselves by erasing the things-in-themselves. Experience thus turns reflexively upon itself and, in the end, comes to know itself for, in the end, that is all there *is* to know. The picture which I offer, in contrast, does not erase things-in-themselves. Rather it recognizes our increasingly adequate epistemological access to them, but recognizes too that in the end whatever laws govern them must govern us as well. For our world is not an aspect of us, but rather we of it. Ultimately, then, knowledge *is* self-knowledge, not for the idealists' reason that there is nothing else to know, but for the deeper reason that to understand what else there is to know — and there is much — we must come to understand our understanding of it.

Only when we have thus reunited ourselves with our world will we, in the fullest sense, have obeyed the Delphic injunction "Know thyself". And is it not, after all, the satisfaction of that imperative which is the final cause of all philosophical activity and which, like all final causes, moves us by its attraction?

NOTES

CHAPTER II

[1] (p. 19) It is not important that one be moved by these counterexamples or, indeed, by any of Kripke's criticisms of Descriptionist views. Shortly I shall be offering a critique of my own, one which supplements such suggestive counterexamples with a more conclusive style of argument.

[2] (p. 23) This is the fundamental observation underlying the variety of examples adduced by Donnellan (*R&DD*) in his discussions of Strawson's views on referring.

CHAPTER III

[1] (p. 37) There is another way to go here as well, of course. One could insist that (1) and (2) are "not fully analyzed". But this is the step which gives rise to the Tractarian notion of "analysis" which was so justifiably attacked by Wittgenstein in the *Philosophical Investigations* as essentially incompletable, and, ultimately, to the paradoxical atomistic ontology of absolute simples which must be present and accounted for if language is to picture the world but of which, curiously, no examples are ever forthcoming. For details, see my *WTLP*.

[2] (p. 39) This gets complicated. There are mixed structure-function kinds: stools, chairs, sofas, loveseats, and so on are distinguished partly on structural grounds. And what about a can-opener so broken that it cannot open cans? What about a *toy* can-opener? The simplest way to look at these cases is as involving the transference of a functional kind-term by analogy. These things are called can-openers because they *were* can-openers or because they *are* structurally quite like things which are, functionally, can-openers.

[3] (p. 41) *Of course* there are other uses of language – questioning, commanding, entreating, and so on. I am concerned with language as a system of representations, however, and so what I wish to get clear about is the use of language to *say how things are.*

[4] (p. 42) A deeper analysis will later reveal this to be a half truth.

[5] (p. 45) This conversation does not apply to the case in which the child is wondering how the pussycat came to be in two pieces.

[6] (p. 46) For the sake of symmetry – and, more importantly, for an adequate theory of intentional action – we must mark language *exits* as well: dispositions to respond to *linguistic* stimuli with *non-linguistic* behavior. Exits are crucial to the understanding of persons, but not to what I am up to at present.

[7] (p. 46) Compare Dennett's fundamental gambit – *C&C*, 39, 'The Way Out'.

[8] (p. 47) The Author is a cousin of Sellars' 'Super inscriber' (*T&C*) and a more distant relative of his 'Omniscient Jones' (*RNWW*).

CHAPTER IV

[1] (p. 54) See Thomson (*PL*), Stroud (*TA*), and Rorty (*VTA*).

[2] (p. 58) This must not be confused with Quine's stronger claim – not here up for discussion – that physical theory is underdetermined by all *possible* observations, all evidence *in principle* intersubjectively available at *any* time. (See, e.g., *W&O*, 22)

[3] (p. 59) Classically, there is nothing much to be said about *how* the data suggest the hypothesis. That forms the putative subject matter of a "logic of discovery". The traditional view is that there can be no such discipline.

[4] (p. 63) A partial listing of central sources: Duhem (*ASPT*); Kuhn (*SSR*); Hanson (*PD*); Feyerabend (*ERE*), (*PE*), (*PE2*); Sellars (*LT*), (*TE*), (*SRII*); and various of the essays in Lakatos and Musgrave (*CGN*).

[5] (p. 66) Deduction certainly enters into the process of explanation – but it is not the deduction of the predecessor laws from the principles of the successor theory. Rather it is typically the deduction of *counterparts* to the predecessor laws within the successor theory under idealizing initial assumptions.

[6] (p. 70) Compare *OR*, 190: "There *seem bound to be* systematically very different ,choices, all of which do justice to all dispositions to verbal behavior on the part of all concerned." (My emphasis.) First, of course, this is not an *argument* but, at best, an appeal to intuitions – intuitions which I do not share. But, second, (and crucially) there is *more* to the acceptability of a set of analytical hypotheses than the question of whether it "does justice to all dispositions to verbal behavior". And once this is recognized, Quine's remark is seen to be beside the point, *even if true.*

CHAPTER V

[1] (p. 75) The question of *entries* to the theoretical language system, whether directly, or by an inferential stop at a "bridge law", "correspondence rule", or "translation rule" may now become acutely troubling. It will be up for discussion shortly.

[2] (p. 76) Something quite like this thesis has been independently defended by Gilbert Harman in a series of essays (*IBE, EI, KIE*), but it is not clear to what extent my considerations run parallel to his.

[3] (p. 76) The account of induction which I am about to offer is largely inspired by Sellars' important essay *IV*, although there are, I suspect, some substantive differences between us.

[4] (p. 78) In the sense of a sample selected *at* random, rather than one selected *to be* random. In the latter sense, 'random' means *representative* and, as my student Anthony Coyne pointed out, a table of random numbers can be accompanied by a list of errata.

[5] (p. 84) For a penetrating critique of the deductive model of explanation, which includes a discussion of this and related questions, see Zaffron, *ISSE*.

[6] (p. 85) That there are *methodological* considerations standing in the way of the *here-and-now* adoption by scientists of the theoretical language, as urged by Feyerabend, has been argued persuasively and at length by Sellars, (*SRII*). The correctness of these points, however, in no way vitiates the *logical* claim which I am here advocating.

[7] (p. 91) I am, unfortunately, constrained to be somewhat dogmatic about Peircean exegesis here. A full defense of this claim would require a careful discussion of the role of Thirdness in Peirce's semiotic and, in particular, a treatment of the principle that every sign is interpreted in a sign. See, for example, his *SCFI*.

[8] (p. 91) Compare Sellars, *S&M*, 101ff.

[9] (p. 93) A more detailed account would see the convergence of absolute numerical values for actual magnitudes of successor theory parameters to the constant value 0 as the reflection of the sequence of correction *functions* required to adjust the counterparts of predecessor laws within successor theories to the new law forms converging to the constant zero *function.*

[10] (p. 94) The correction *factors*, of course, converge in the Weierstrass sense to the known value 0. It is the sequence of *theories* which can, by implication, be then said to converge toward an ideal Peircean limit theory in a sense modeled on the Cauchy convergence of numerical sequences.

CHAPTER VI

[1] (p. 101) There is a modest complication introduced by the fact that the feature, φ', in virtue of which X portrays and the feature, ψ, in virtue of which X indefinitely indicates enter asymmetrically into the account. One is content; the other, form. Thus, for example, it is a Q-shaped patch of red pigment, *not* a red patch of Q-shaped pigment. 'Red' marks content; 'Q-shaped' marks form. A great deal is buried under this observation, but it would lead us too far afield for me to pursue the matter here. For a beginning exploration of the consequences of the distinction, see my *RFOS* and *GHTI*.

[2] (p. 102) Wilfrid Sellars finally convinced me that I ought to do this. It was hard work on his part, but don't blame him. He was right.

[3] (p. 103) Dispensing with the expository device of pair-objects, we could here put:

> (Objects) *a* and *b* indicate (cities) A and B and portray the former as being to the west of the latter by being respectively the one to the left of the other.

[4] (p. 104) This is not quite right, because the asymmetry of content and form marked earlier does correspond to a genuine and important difference between *kinds* and *characteristics* in the represented world, but it is close enough for present purposes.

[5] (p. 106) Compare Strawson (*P*, 134): "The idea of a predicate is correlative with that of a range of distinguishable individuals of which the predicate can be significantly, though not necessarily truly, affirmed."

[6] (p. 116) Triadic concatenation can be built up out of dyadic concatenation according to the recursive rule:

$$\text{concat3}\#\langle a,b,c\rangle = \text{concat2}\#\langle a,b\rangle \ \& \ \text{concat2}\#\langle\langle a,b\rangle,c\rangle$$

CHAPTER VII

[1] (p. 129) I have articulated many of these difficulties in my *RNF*.

[2] (p. 132) There are, of course, other inferential patterns facilitating the introduction of disjunctions as well, a leading example of which might be:

> p or not p
> if p then q
> if not p then r
> Therefore, q or r

[3] (p. 132) These observations have profound implications for our understanding of the concept of a person and for what has been called "the ethics of belief". What is at stake here is the essential unity of the concept of a person – the concept of a single entity which is both knower (and thus subject to epistemic appraisal) and doer (and so a fit subject of moral assessment). Fundamental questions in the metaphysics of morals turn on the demonstrability of this unitary character of our person-concept. I hope on some later occasion to explore these matters fully, but, unfortunately, I have neither time nor space (nor yet sufficient insight) to do more than open the topic here.

[4] (p. 135) To mention two obvious examples: I have had nothing to say about indexicality and personal pronouns and nothing to say about the critical matters of time and tense. I have skimmed a chip off of each of these icebergs elsewhere. For indexicality, see my *IST*; for time, *BTSS* and *OWUT*.

CHAPTER VIII

[1] (p. 136) I take as central documents here Wittgenstein's *PI* and Strawson's *I*. The revolution reaches maturity with Strawson's *BS*, Bennett's *KA*, and Sellars' *S&M*.

[2] (p. 136) J.J. Thomson, *PL*; Stroud, *TA*; Rorty, *VTA*

[3] (p. 136) See e.g., Sellars' *EPM*, Feyerabend's *ERE*, and the essay by Lakatos in Lakatos and Musgrave, *CGN*, as well as my own *GHTI*, for some representative examples.

[4] (p. 145) How *might* it go? Well, the universe contains energy sources and systems of elements into which energy is continually pumped. The laws of the universe imply that a system into which energy is thus continuously fed will evolve to increasingly higher stages of organization (this is *now* known) — simple molecules, nucleic acids, cells, multi-cellular organisms, organisms with functionally differentiated organic parts, and so on. We can see the emergence of an integrative representational consciousness as a late stage of this general integrative evolutionary process. For the other side of the coin, we look at a universe which in fact contains physical systems thus highly integrated and observe that only such an evolutionary process could result in the presence of such systems. If we then tease out the physical preconditions of energy flux having integrative consequences, we may well find that certain extremely general and fundamental physical features of the universe — e.g., such "very large numbers" as the ratio of electromagnetic to gravitational force; the three-dimensionality of space; and the basic conservation principles — are among those preconditions.

BIBLIOGRAPHY

Aldrich, Virgil, (IS), 'Illocutionary Space', *Philosophy and Phenomenological Research* 82 (1971), 15–28.

Alston, William P., (M&U), 'Meaning and Use', *Philosophical Quarterly* 12, (1963), 107–24. Reprinted as pp. 403–419 of Rosenberg and Travis, *RPL*.

Aune, Bruce, (KM&N), *Knowledge, Mind and Nature*, Random House, New York, 1967.

Austin, J.L. (HDTW), *How to Do Things With Words*, Oxford University Press, Oxford, 1962.

Bennett, Jonathan, (KA), *Kant's Analytic*, Cambridge University Press, Cambridge, 1966.

Carroll, Lewis, 'What the Tortoise Said to Achilles', *Mind* 4, (1895), 278–80. Variously reprinted.

Chomsky, Noam, (ATS), *Aspects of the Theory of Syntax*, MIT Press, Cambridge, Mass., 1965.

Davidson, Donald (T&M), 'Truth and Meaning', *Synthese* 17, (1967), 304–23. Reprinted as pp. 450–65 of Rosenberg and Travis, *RPL*.

Dennett, D.C., (C&C), *Content and Consciousness*, Humanities Press, New York, 1969.

Donnellan, Keith S., (R&DD), 'Reference and Definite Descriptions', *The Philosophical Review* 75, (1966), 281–304.

Duhem, Pierre, (ASPT), *The Aim and Structure of Physical Theory*, translated by Philip P. Wiener, Princeton University Press, Princeton, N.J., 1954.

Feigl, Herbert, and Grover Maxwell (eds.), (CIPS), *Current Issues in the Philosophy of Science*, Holt, Rinehart and Winston, New York, 1961.

Feyerabend, Paul K., (ERE), 'Explanation, Reduction and Empiricism', pp. 28–97 of *Minnesota Studies in the Philosophy of Science*, Vol. III (ed. by H. Feigl and G. Maxwell), University of Minnesota Press, Minneapolis, 1962.

Feyerabend, Paul K., (PE), 'Problems of Empiricism', pp. 145–260 of *Beyond the Edge of Certainty* (ed. by R.G. Colodny), Prentice-Hall, Inc., Englewood Cliffs, N.J., 1965.

Feyerabend, Paul K., (PE2), 'Problems of Empiricism, Part 2', pp. 275–354 of *The Nature and Function of Scientific Theories* (ed. by R.G. Colodny), University of Pittsburgh Press, Pittsburgh, 1970.

Geach, Peter (MA), *Mental Acts*, Routledge and Kegan Paul, London, 1957.

Goodman, Nelson, (LA), *Languages of Art*, Bobbs-Merrill, Indianapolis and New York, 1968.

Grice, H.P., (M), 'Meaning', *Philosophical Review* 66, (1957), 377–88. Reprinted as pp. 436–44 of Rosenberg and Travis, *RPL*.

Grice, H.P., (UMI), 'Utterer's Meaning and Intentions', *Philosophical Review* 78, (1969), 147–77.

Hanson, Norwood Russell, (ILSD), 'Is There a Logic of Scientific Discovery?' in Feigl and Maxwell, *CIPS*.

Hanson, Norwood Russell, (PD), *Patterns of Discovery*, Cambridge University Press, Cambridge, 1958.

Harman, Gilbert, (EI), 'Enumerative Induction as Inference to the Best Explanation', *Journal of Philosophy* 65, (1968), 529–33.

Harman, Gilbert, (*IBE*), 'Inference to the Best Explanation', *Philosophical Review* 74, (1965), 88–95.

Harman, Gilbert, (*KIE*), 'Knowledge, Inference and Explanation', *American Philosophical Quarterly* 5, (1968), 164–73.

Harman, Gilbert and Donald Davidson (eds.), (*SNL*), *Semantics of Natural Language*, D. Reidel, Dordrecht, Holland, 1972.

Hempel, C.G. and Paul Oppenheim, (*LE*), 'The Logic of Explanation', *Philosophy of Science* 15, (1948). Reprinted as pp. 319–52 of *Readings in the Philosophy of Science* (ed. by Herbert Feigl and May Brodbeck), Appleton-Century-Crofts, New York, 1953.

Kneale, William, (*P&I*), *Probability and Induction*, Oxford University Press, Oxford, 1949.

Kripke, Saul, (*I&N*), 'Identity and Necessity', pp. 135–164 of *Identity and Individuation* (edited by Milton K. Munitz), New York University Press, New York, 1971.

Kripke, Saul, (*NN*), 'Naming and Necessity', pp. 253–355 of Harman and Davidson, *SNL*.

Kuhn, Thomas, (*SSR*), *The Structure of Scientific Revolutions*, University of Chicago Press, Chicago, 1962.

Lakatos, Imre, and Alan Musgrave, eds., (*CGK*), *Criticism and the Growth of Knowledge*, Cambridge University Press, Cambridge, 1970.

Peirce, C.S., (*A&I*), 'Abduction and Induction', Chapter 11, pp. 150–56 of Peirce, *PRP*.

Peirce, C.S., (*FB*), 'The Fixation of Belief', Chapter 2, pp. 5–22 of Peirce, *PRP*.

Peirce, C.S., (*HMIC*), 'How to Make Our Ideas Clear', Chapter 3, pp. 23–41 of Peirce, *PRP*.

Peirce, C.S., (*PRP*), *Philosophical Writings of Peirce* (ed. by Justus Buchler), Dover Publications, New York, 1955.

Peirce, C.S., (*SCFI*), 'Some Consequences of Four Incapacities', Chapter 16, pp. 228–50 of Peirce, *PRP*.

Pitcher, George, (*IT*), 'Introduction' in *Truth*, Prentice-Hall, Inc., Englewood Cliffs, N.J., 1964.

Plato, (*T*), *Theatetus* (transl. by Francis M. Cornford), *Plato's Theory of Knowledge*, Bobbs-Merrill, Indianapolis and New York, 1957.

Quine, Willard Van Orman, (*LPV*), *From a Logical Point of View*, Harper and Row, New York and Evanston, 1963.

Quine, Willard Van Orman, (*OR*), 'Ontological Relativity', *Journal of Philosophy* 65, (1968), 185–212.

Quine, Willard Van Orman, (*OWTI*), 'On What There Is', Chapter 1, pp. 1–19, of Quine, *LPV*.

Quine, Willard Van Orman, (*TDE*), 'Two Dogmas of Empiricism', Chapter 2, pp. 20–46 of Quine, *LPV*.

Quine, Willard Van Orman, (*W&O*), *Word and Object*, MIT Press, Cambridge, Mass., 1960.

Ramsey, Frank P., (*FM*), *The Foundations of Mathematics*, Routledge and Kegan Paul, London, 1931. Reissued in paper by Littlefield, Adams and Co., Paterson, N.J., 1960.

Rorty, Richard, (*VTA*), 'Verificationism and Transcendental Arguments', *Nous* 5, (1971), 3–14.

Rorty, Richard, (*WWL*), 'The World Well Lost', *Journal of Philosophy* 69, (1972), 649–65.

Rosenberg, Jay F., (*BTSS*), 'Bergmann on Time – Showing and Saying', *Mind* 77, (1968), 279–87.

Rosenberg, Jay F., (*GHTI*), 'The "Given" and How to Take It – Some Reflections on

Phenomenal Ontology', *Metaphilosophy*, forthcoming.

Rosenberg, Jay F., (*IST*), 'Intentionality and Self in the *Tractatus*', *Nous* 2, (1968), 341–58.

Rosenberg, Jay F., (*NPT*), 'New Perspectives on the *Tractatus*', *Dialogue* 4, (1966), 506–17.

Rosenberg, Jay F., (*OWUT*), 'One Way of Understanding Time', *Philosophia* 2, (1972), 283–301.

Rosenberg, Jay F., (*RFOS*), 'Russell and the Form of Outer Sense', in *Bertrand Russell – A Memorial Symposium*, Vol. I (ed. by George W. Roberts), George Allen & Unwin, Ltd., forthcoming.

Rosenberg, Jay F., (*RNF*), 'Russell on Negative Facts', *Nous* 6, (1972), 27–40.

Rosenberg, Jay F., (*SEL*), 'Synonymy and the Epistemology of Linguistics', *Inquiry* 10, (1967), 405–20.

Rosenberg, Jay F., (*WSC*), 'Wittgenstein's Self-Criticisms *or* "Whatever Happened to the Picture Theory?" ', *Nous* 4, (1970), 209–23.

Rosenberg, Jay F., (*WTLP*), 'Wittgenstein's Theory of Language as Picture', *American Philosophical Quarterly* 5, (1968), 18–30.

Rosenberg, Jay F. and Charles Travis (eds.), (*RPL*), *Readings in the Philosophy of Language*, Prentice-Hall, Inc., Englewood Cliffs, N.J., 1971.

Russell, Bertrand, (*L&K*), *Logic and Knowledge* (ed. by Robert C. Marsh), The Macmillan Company, 1956.

Russell, Bertrand, (*OP*), 'On Propositions: What They Are and How They Mean', pp. 283–320 of Russell, *L&K*.

Russell, Bertrand, (*PLA*), 'The Philosophy of Logical Atomism', pp. 175–282 of Russell, *L&K*.

Ryle, Gilbert, (*CM*), *The Concept of Mind*, Barnes and Noble, Inc., New York, 1949.

Searle, John R., (*SpA*), *Speech Acts*, Cambridge University Press, Cambridge, 1969.

Sellars, Wilfrid, (*AE*), 'Abstract Entities', Chapter IX, pp. 229–269 of Sellars, *PP*.

Sellars, Wilfrid, (*B&BK*), 'Being and Being Known', Chapter 2, pp. 41–59 of Sellars, *SPR*.

Sellars, Wilfrid, (*EPM*), 'Empiricism and the Philosophy of Mind', Chapter 5, pp. 112–96 of Sellars, *SPR*.

Sellars, Wilfrid, (*IV*), 'Induction as Vindication', *Philosophy of Science* 31, (1964), 197–231.

Sellars, Wilfrid, (*LT*), 'The Language of Theories', Chapter 4, pp. 106–126 of Sellars, *SPR*.

Sellars, Wilfrid, (*LTC*), 'Language as Thought and Communication', *Philosophy and Phenomenological Research* 29, (1969), pp. 506–27.

Sellars, Wilfrid, (*N&S*), 'Naming and Saying', Chapter 7, pp. 225–46 of Sellars, *SPR*.

Sellars, Wilfrid, (*PP*), *Philosophical Perspectives*, Charles C. Thomas, Publisher, Springfield, Illinois, 1967.

Sellars, Wilfrid, (*RNWW*), 'Realism and the New Way of Words', *Philosophy and Phenomenological Research* 8, (1948). Reprinted as pp. 424–456 of *Readings in Philosophical Analysis* (ed. by H. Feigl and W. Sellars), Appleton-Century-Crofts, New York, 1949.

Sellars, Wilfrid, (*S&M*), *Science and Metaphysics*, Routledge and Kegan Paul, London, 1968.

Sellars, Wilfrid, (*SPR*), *Science, Perception and Reality*, Routledge and Kegan Paul, London, 1963.

Sellars, Wilfrid, (*SRII*), 'Scientific Realism or Irenic Instrumentalism', Chapter XIV, pp. 337–69 of Sellars, *PP*.

Sellars, Wilfrid, (*SRLG*), 'Some Reflections on Language Games', Chapter 11, pp. 321–58 of Sellars, *SPR*.

Sellars, Wilfrid, (*T&C*), 'Truth and "Correspondence"', Chapter 6, pp. 197–224 of Sellars, *SPR*.

Sellars, Wilfrid, (*TE*), 'Theoretical Explanation', Chapter XIII, pp. 321–336 of Sellars, *PP*.

Snyder, Aaron, (*RL*), 'Rules of Language', *Mind* 80, (1971), 161–78.

Strawson, P.F., (*BS*), *The Bounds of Sense*, Methuen and Co., Ltd., London, 1966.

Strawson, P.F., (*I*), *Individuals*, Methuen and Co., Ltd., London, 1959.

Strawson, P.F., (*OR*), 'On Referring', *Mind* 59, 1950, pp. 320–344. Reprinted as pp. 175–95 of Rosenberg and Travis, *RPL*.

Strawson, P.F., (*P*), 'Persons', *Minnesota Studies in the Philosophy of Science* (ed. by H. Feigl, M. Scriven, and G. Maxwell), University of Minnesota Press, Minneapolis, 1958. Reprinted as pp. 127–46 of *The Philosophy of Mind* (ed. by V.C. Chappell), Prentice-Hall, Inc., Englewood Cliffs, N.J., 1962.

Stroud, Barry (*TA*); 'Transcendental Arguments', *Journal of Philosophy* 65, (1968), 241–56.

Thomson, Judith Jarvis, (*PL*), 'Private Languages', *Americal Philosophical Quarterly* 1, (1964), 20–31.

Toulmin, Stephen, (*F&U*), *Foresight and Understanding*, Indiana University Press, Bloomington, Ind., 1961.

Wittgenstein, Ludwig, (*N*), *Notebooks 1914–1916* (ed. and transl. by G.E.M. Anscombe and G.H. Von Wright), Harper and Brothers, New York, 1961.

Wittgenstein, Ludwig, (*PI*), *Philosophical Investigations* (transl. by G.E.M. Anscombe), The Macmillan Company, New York, 1953.

Wittgenstein, Ludwig, (*TLP*), *Tractatus Logico-Philosophicus* (transl. by D.F. Pears and B.F. McGuinness), Routledge and Kegan Paul, London, 1961.

Zaffron, Richard, (*ISSE*), 'Identity, Subsumption and Scientific Explanation', *Journal of Philosophy* 68, (1971), 849–60.

Ziff, Paul, (*SA*), *Semantic Analysis*, Cornell University Press, Ithaca, N.Y., 1960.

INDEX OF NAMES

INDEX OF SUBJECTS